EAST END HEROES, STATESIDE KINGS

BRIAN BELTON

EAST END HEROES, STATESIDE KINGS

The Story of West Ham United's
Three Claret, Blue and
Black Pioneers

JOHN BLAKE

John Blake Publishing
Published by John Blake Publishing Ltd,
3 Bramber Court, 2 Bramber Road,
London W14 9PB, England

www.blake.co.uk

First published in hardback in 2008

ISBN: 978 1 84454 501 8

British Library Cataloguing-in-Publication Data:

A catalogue record for this book is available from the British Library.

Design by www.envydesign.co.uk

Printed in Great Britain by William Clowes Ltd, Beccles, Suffolk

1 3 5 7 9 10 8 6 4 2

Papers used by John Blake Publishing are natural, recyclable products
made from wood grown in sustainable forests. The manufacturing processes
conform to the environmental regulations of the country of origin.

Every attempt has been made to contact the relevant copyright-holders,
but some were unobtainable. We would be grateful if the appropriate
people could contact us.

This book is dedicated to the Ebony Dawn of the spring of 1972.
It is written in remembrance and appreciation of the life and work of Clive Charles.

'Black or white, football is under all our skins.'

EUSÉBIO

*'The soccer ball doesn't care what colour you are...
black or white, we were all mates.'*

CLYDE BEST

*'Britain and America are two nations divided by a
common language.'*

WINSTON CHURCHILL, GEORGE BERNARD SHAW
AND OSCAR WILDE

Author's note: Given the context of this book, the words 'soccer' and 'football' have been used interchangeably.

CONTENTS

INTRODUCTION

This is a book that focuses on the life stories of three men, reflecting on their profession and its place in their wider lives. At the same time, it seeks to tell at least something of the context of those lives. Of course, their stories begin where all our biographies start, at different points in history and in different places. In the case of our East End heroes, one does indeed begin in the East End of London; another starts close to a thousand miles north of the Caribbean, and the other has its roots in Africa. But, from these very diverse environments, they were united for a significant period of their lives. That moment was at 3.00pm on 1 April 1972; the place was Upton Park. They all wore the claret-and-blue shirts of West Ham United Football Club.

The same scenario today would not be unusual at all, but more than a third of a century ago it was uncommon for an English football club in the top flight of the game to include such a cosmopolitan element in a starting XI, at a time when the most likely 'foreigners' in the English game were from Scotland, Ireland or Wales. So, names like Dick Kryswicki, Asa Hartford and Eamonn Dunphy were the most 'exotic' that your average 1970s supporter would come across. However, it was even more out of the ordinary – in fact, it was unique – for a team in Division One of the Football League to field three black players, but, on that day in 1972, that is what West Ham's manager Ron Greenwood did.

I have written about the lives of all West Ham's black players up to the 2006 FA Cup Final and, of course, included Ade Coker, Clyde Best and Clive Charles, but there was something quite unique about these 'Onyx Odins' that requires elaboration and further analysis. The biographies of this history-making trio before that match tell us much about society in general, and the state of the game at that time. They had all been drawn to football when they were young, hardly more than boys, and found themselves on the same pitch, fighting for the cause of one of football's most romantic and enigmatic clubs.

What happened to them after that match is even more fascinating and has become a significant part of our sporting and social history. Without really being conscious of the fact at the time, Coker, Best and Charles broke through a barrier in the English game, in a collective way that was not to be repeated for years.

But there was more pioneering to come. In the space of the same decade, these three East End heroes 'crossed the pond' and, in different ways, helped build the American soccer dream, playing a major part in helping to kick-start the National American Soccer League. Other former West Ham players were similarly significant pioneers in the development of the American League, such as Phil Woosnam, Bobby Howe and Bobby Moore, but the collective impact of the 'Black Hammers' of 1972 was both explosive and had an impact right across the Americas, from Portland to California, from Toronto to Bermuda. One would even wear the American Eagle over his heart as an international player; another would coach the USA to unprecedented Olympic achievement and domination in the female game; and Clyde Best would begin to build a soccer nation.

These were the men who first inspired me to leave behind the gang and street life of the East End, where I was born and brought up, in favour of a more meaningful and productive path. They were the individuals I watched from afar, either from Upton Park's North Bank (now the Centenary Stand) or on a Saturday evening/Sunday afternoon on the television. When I eventually met them, I could not believe, even as a mature adult, that they were talking to me.

I have also tried to capture something of the history that created this trio, and to explore their individual paths to fame and recognition, and the places that they plied their trade and where they ended up. In undertaking this task, I have attempted to show the nature of what it is that they helped to build – the chronicle of American soccer. This same history has involved the development of a number of influential coaches and managers both in England and America, and also serves as a testament to the contribution of West Ham United to the development of the game in the USA. In turn, this soccer revolution fed back into the game in the UK through the players who were advantaged by working with two of the Hammers' greatest managers - John Lyall and Ron Greenwood. I have also given space to looking at the influence of men like Woosnam and Howe, and other Hammers who influenced them, such as Harry Redknapp, John Bond and Ken Brown. They themselves had been inspired by another Boleyn Ground generation, led by Noel Cantwell and Malcolm Allison.

It is hard for us today to imagine what it took to convert 'football' to 'soccer' and transplant it in a nation that had so much resistance to it; which had, in fact, successfully killed it many times previously. Tremendous amounts of money and a huge effort was expended to 'make soccer happen' in the only land it had never conquered. The birth, growth and development of the National American Soccer League (NASL), and its relationship to what went before and after, is a fascinating tale in itself. But to understand Charles, Best and Coker, their challenges and achievement, one has to have some awareness of how the NASL and its clubs came into being and try to understand its demise. In many ways, it helped to make legends of those three Black Hammers; their involvement with it helped create what it is today, and thus they have played a crucial role in the bringing of football to the consciousness of the American people.

Over the years I have spent putting this book together - it is over 30 years since I first talked to Clive Charles - I have become ever more conscious of the contribution of the

African diaspora to the development and progression of humanity as a whole. This book acts as a reminder of the gift of those people who found themselves bound together by oppression and love, a newfound liberation and a constant resistance to hatred. As such, the wisdom of those lives extends far beyond the white boundaries of a football pitch.

East End Heroes, Stateside Kings is published at a moment when British society celebrates its 200-year march away from slavery and its abandonment of that malevolent institution that betrayed shackled black people and utterly demeaned and dehumanised the whites who profited from that shameful trade. The book has been published at this time partly to highlight the extraordinary achievements of those who were part of that movement of black people from slavery to freedom over the last two centuries, and to demonstrate how far we have come. The passage, though, despite these more enlightened times, is far from over.

What follows explores identity, struggle, pain, frustration, loss and courage – the stuff that makes East End heroes. But it is also an examination of the indomitable spirit that enables us to endure hardship, turn it around and then drive on to success. This spirit, I think, had begun to grow in those three young 'Champions of Spring', back in the early days of the optimistic 1970s; it was the fountainhead of the energy, intelligence and commitment that would make them Stateside Kings.

1

WEST HAM UNITED

Even before the move towards more leisure, the people
of West Ham, at the extreme easterly end of London's
Docklands, on the western edge of the county of Essex,
had one true love – West Ham United. Although the
district of West Ham took many sports to its heart and
nurtured champions in most, the area's greatest passion
has always been football. To understand West Ham, one
needs to comprehend something of the history of the
club that has become synonymous with the community
that surrounds it.

It is probably fair to say that few other sporting institutions
are so thoroughly intermeshed with their local communities
as West Ham United. The birthplace of the Hammers, an
organisation existing primarily to play a game, has radically
influenced the culture of the club. At the same time, the
institutional cause of the 'Irons' has radiated out into the East

End of London and has been part of its evolution. The district itself has moulded the club in its own image, while the club has helped to shape the area; it is a unique symbiotic relationship – West Ham, the soccer club, and the broad expanse of East London and West Essex, are one. That oneness is claret and blue, and lives under the symbol of two crossed hammers.

No one knows where and when soccer started but, in 1848, some interested and enthused men at Cambridge University refined the rules of the game as it was then played, probably fairly violently, by the working classes. The Football Association was founded in England in 1863 for the express purpose of codifying the rules, and the world's first International, between England and Scotland, took place in 1872.

In 1885, professionalism was legalised and, in 1888, the Football League was formed with 12 clubs: Accrington, Aston Villa, Blackburn Rovers, Bolton Wanderers, Burnley, Derby County, Everton, Notts County, Preston North End, Stoke, West Bromwich Albion and Wolverhampton Wanderers. All were from the North or Midlands. Fifteen years later, in 1900, West Ham United was born.

But the origins of West Ham can be traced back years earlier as the works team of Thames Ironworks, a shipyard on the bank of the Thames, down-river from central and West London, which specialised in building iron ships. Arnold Hills, the owner, had been educated at Harrow and Oxford, and had played football for England against Scotland in 1879. He was very keen on the health of his workers (as well as diverting them from union activity, the kind that, a few years earlier, had given rise to one of the greatest dock strikes in history), and in 1895 he built a sports complex that cost £20,000, a massive sum at the time, with a cycle track and a football pitch. That first season, on their new pitch, the Thames Ironworks team managed to play some evening matches under floodlight by stringing electric light-bulbs from poles and dipping the ball in whitewash to make it more visible. It was noted that, when the Ironworks were about to shoot, the lights seemed, miraculously, to dim, making it much harder for the opposing goalkeeper.

In 1898, Thames were promoted to the respectable Southern League, but a bit of wheeling and dealing had been going on, unbeknown to Hills, and the side were fined £25 by the Football Association. Their crime had been to hire an agent to tempt players away from the Football League.

Once the Ironworks were in the Southern League, they ceased to be a purely works team, although they had hardly ever been that. They were employing semi-professionals and were soon looking for a ground that might draw better crowds, as lack of support threatened the continuation of the side as a profit-making entity. Arnold Hills realised that he could no longer finance the club from his own pocket, as he didn't want such a close affiliation with distasteful professionalism. On 5 July 1900, a new company was formed called West Ham Football Club, named after the borough within which it was founded, with a capital of £2,000, to be raised by selling 4,000 ten-shilling shares. The team's colours, from its beginnings as Thames Ironworks, had been Oxford blue, the house colours of the shipyard, but it was to

3

become claret and blue, probably to be associated with Aston Villa, the Birmingham-based side who were very successful at that time.[1] The crossed hammers on the club's badge came from the shipyard, representing riveting hammers, and not from the name West Ham,[2] which is what many modern fans wrongly imagine. Even now supporters still shout in support, 'Come on, you Irons' as much as 'Go on, you Hammers!'

In 1904, West Ham United moved to the Boleyn Ground, Upton Park. The ground had good railway connections but, more importantly, it was away from premises controlled by Hills, a vegetarian, teetotal Christian, who was dead set against gambling, one of the main reasons men (and it was more or less all men) attended soccer matches. From then on, it seemed that the team had two home grounds, for as many people who refer to West Ham's 'Upton Park home', others say that the Hammers play at the 'Boleyn Ground', and some refer to both. The name Boleyn came from a local house where Anne Boleyn (the second of Henry VIII's six wives) is supposed to have stayed for a time.

Until 1902, West Ham had been subsidised by Hills, but that year they acquired manager Syd King and became much more of an independent entity. Although a Southern League club (not one of the elite members of the Football League), West Ham always managed good FA Cup runs (the Football

---

1. There is a story that the shirts were stitched together out of scraps, the arms being blue and the rest of the shirt a claret red, but this seems to be a tale forged by wishes for West Ham not to be seen as 'plagiarists' of any sort.

2. 'Ham' is actually old English for 'Island' or 'settlement' related to a small holding. West Ham was, in pre-modern times, a marsh-land district, situated on the 'flats' of the Thames

Association Cup was the biggest and is still the oldest soccer competition in the world). In 1905, they lost to Woolwich Arsenal (who would later become simply 'Arsenal') and, in 1907, they reached the third round, drawn at home against the mighty Newcastle United. Newcastle offered the Hammers £1,000 in cash to play the match at the North-Easterners' home ground of St James' Park, but West Ham refused. They drew 0-0 at Upton Park but lost the replay on Tyneside. In 1913, the Irons lost at home to Aston Villa in the second round. From an attendance of 50,000, the gate receipts were £2,000, a terrific sum for the time.

After the First World War, West Ham, having gained a good record playing against much bigger clubs during the war, were elected into the Football League, joining the Second Division. They were in such a hurry to sign on to the League that they broke Southern League rules and were fined £500.

Great glory came to West Ham United in 1923. For many reasons, the FA Cup Final of that year made history, not just for West Ham fans but for most people in England. It was the first time the Final had been played at the new Wembley Stadium, which had been built at a cost of £750,000 as the focal point of the 1924–25 British Empire Exhibition. In the Final match programme, Wembley was described as '... *the Greatest Arena in the world, the largest, the most comfortable, the best equipped... In area, it equals the Biblical City of Jericho.*'

It was also the so-called 'White Horse' Cup Final, a legend in its own right. Wembley had been built to accommodate 127,000 people, but about twice as many turned up for the

Final between West Ham and Bolton Wanderers. Many managed somehow to get in, which meant that there were around 250,000 within the stadium. Trying to save themselves from being crushed or suffocated, people spilled on to the pitch, where there was soon chaos until, as the legend goes, Police Constable Storey, on his white horse, restored some order, saving hundreds from being trampled to death. The scenes were captured on film but then, as now, there had been a lot of jostling beforehand for the right to record the event. Pathe News did not win it but they sneaked a cameraman into the stadium disguised as a West Ham supporter. He was carrying a large cardboard hammer, under which he held his camera. In fact, there was no white horse. The creature captured on film was a dirty grey beast, one of many at the event. After the game, West Ham coach Charlie Paynter would blame the state of the turf after the trampling of the many police-horse hooves, as being responsible for making the playing surface difficult for his side, who relied on service from the wings, the area of the pitch most affected by the 'ploughing'. Possibly, as a result, West Ham lost 2–0.

It was not until 1940 that West Ham supporters would truly receive a triumph worthy of their support. The War Cup Final that year was held at Wembley and West Ham qualified to play Blackburn Rovers. Like Bolton in 1923, Blackburn was another long-established northern club, founded in 1875, who had won the Cup five times in the 1880s and 1890s. Alfred Wainwright, later famous for his guidebooks to the Lakeland fells, was a co-founder and chairman of the

Blackburn Rovers Supporters' Club. He came down by coach for the Final, and saw West Ham win 1-0 before a crowd of 42,399. It was West Ham's first 'major' trophy.

Later, the club would build a reputation as a place that developed talent. In 1950, Bobby Moore, aged only 17, made his first-team debut, replacing the club captain, Malcolm Allison, who was recovering from a spell in a TB sanatorium. In the following season, Moore made only three appearances, but would go on to become one of England's greatest football and sporting heroes.

During this period, manager Ron Greenwood's three star players were all home-grown - Moore, Martin Peters and Geoff Hurst. Another was John Charles. He captained the first West Ham team to win the FA Youth Cup in 1963, to become the first black player to skipper a team to victory in an important peacetime national tournament. In March of the same year, Greenwood made him the first black player to take the field as part of a West Ham first team.

In 1964, West Ham defeated Manchester United in the FA Cup Semi-Final, and went on to beat Preston North End in the Final, 3-2; this made the Hammers the last side made up entirely of Englishmen to play in all rounds of the FA Cup up to the Final and win. That year, Bobby Moore was named Footballer of the Year. At last, West Ham supporters had something to provoke mass celebrations and there was a victory parade several miles long through the heart of London's East End.

In 1965, the team went on to win the European Cup Winners' Cup, only the second English club to take a European trophy; Tottenham Hotspur, the Hammers' North London rivals, had won the Cup Winners' Cup two years earlier, but with a side made up of men coming from all over the British Isles and captained by Danny Blanchflower, an Irishman. West Ham were the first all-English XI to win a European trophy, with most of the team being born within a few miles of the Boleyn Ground. Hence, the Hammers became 'The First and Last Englishmen'.

West Ham have always been known for their lack of consistency – periods of flair, elegance and success have often been followed by barren times ending in relegation. Sometimes, they have lived up to the title the 'Academy of Football', a name by which the club is known nationally, giving lessons in style and tactics. At other periods in its history, the team seems to have been comprised of solid but limited artisans. For all this, West Ham have been unusual in that, during their first 90 years, they had called on the services of just five managers. And, until the 1990s, they were consistently a local team, drawing their support and most of their players from their immediate catchment area. Other London clubs like Arsenal, Spurs and Chelsea have always been cosmopolitan, glamorous, big-city institutions, attracting support and stars from all over the country and beyond. By comparison, West Ham have been loved and supported locally, although they have fan outposts in nearly every country of the world. Very often, as in the 1964 Cup Final, they have put out a team that was not just totally English but also heavily local, with most members coming from East London or the neighbouring county of Essex. At its most popular, the team could attract close to half-a-million supporters over a season's home games.

West Ham United has become a means of identity for what was and is a population with massively diverse roots; the club brought people together within one claret-and-blue community. What started as a diversion peppered with the spice of gambling became something that said this is 'us' – the 'we' of support melded a community of followers. The singing of the Hammers theme song, 'I'm Forever Blowing Bubbles', a melancholic 'wanting tune', premised on the need for hopes and dreams by the tens of thousands of supporters crushed into the Boleyn Ground, has resonated around the East End for generations and has become an anthem for the area. In the mid-20th century, young women making their way home after the afternoon shift from the Lesney toy factory would pour out in their hundreds across Hackney Marshes, arms linked, singing; babies in their cribs about to stir in the back yards of the tightly packed Dockland terraces would be lulled back into sleep by the lullaby; down on the river, brave little tugs would hoot in chorus as the passengers on the Woolwich ferry took up the melody. Within seconds, the whole of the teeming masses of the East End would vibrate to a harmonious claret-and-blue emotion that marked 'our' presence – the Water People, North of the River, East of the Tower!

This is the environment that Clive Charles was born into, and that Clyde Best and Ade Coker came to. Three young men from Canning Town, Africa and an island in the warm Atlantic Ocean, seemingly almost totally dissimilar in background and character, were 'United' in the passion of Dockland identity and one of the great sources of solace in a place and time wracked by war and poverty.

For the best part of 250 years, the West Ham district has been one of the poorest in Britain. It was trounced by the Nazi Blitz of the 1940s. As a boy, in the 1960s, my friends and I were still playing on bombsites from that time. Indeed, it was in such places that we first kicked a ball. Although the borough has always been a melting pot in terms of its ethnic make-up, being close to the docks, the centre of world trade, quite unfairly at times, it has often been associated with racism. However, this view was magnified by the popular comedy soap opera *Till Death Us Do Part* that was viewed by tens of millions of Britons from the 1960s. The show's main character was the controversial Alf Garnett, an ignorant, West Ham-supporting, Cockney racist that the writer, a man from the West Ham area, Johnny Speight, a traditional socialist, sought to use to lampoon some of the worst aspects of British society. However, for most people, Alf was perceived as the epitome of East London culture and the satire that was delivered in an almost documentary style became, for many, a truth. And so, a long tradition of anti-racism and diversity that marked the East End out, for all its problems, as one of the most accepting of areas in terms of race and ethnicity was wiped out by a weekly half-hour TV show that was written with those very traditions as a backdrop.

West Ham United fans became associated with racism and were consistently used as exemplars of the worst type of supporters. Of course, there have been those who have 'jumped on the bandwagon' and made profit from the image, but, as a person who has supported the Hammers since the late 1950s and who has interviewed over a hundred former and current players, and many thousands of fans, I can only say that the picture is one contorted by a strange alliance of the popular media and sections of the most virulently over-compensating 'chattering classes'. Many of these social 'commentators' have been quick to be seen to condemn what has become an easy target and, by that, distance themselves from deeper and more complex issues that feed racism in society.

West Ham United reached the FA Cup Final for the fifth time in 2006. Nigel Reo Coker captained a side that was truly multi-racial, made up of young men from all over the world, but there was still a core of Londoners and one or two who had supported West Ham as boys. For many years, the club has been active in the 'Kick It Out' campaign that looks to eradicate racism from football, and the Hammers continue to lead the way in terms of promotion of the great resource that Britain has in its diversity, which can only be fully realised when channelled into a commonality of aim and purpose. But the fact that West Ham were one of the forerunners in this movement has been forgotten. The contribution of the likes of John Charles has been ignored, as well as that moment when three black players took the field for West Ham, long before any other first-class club achieved this milestone. Years later, Midlands club West Bromwich Albion would become well known for 'The Three

Degrees' – Brendon Batson, Cyrille Regis and the fantastically talented East Londoner Laurie Cunningham – but West Ham did it first. Not only that, but the three black young men who ran out at Upton Park on 1 April 1972 went on to help build the world game for more than 30 years; they were pioneers, heroes and kings.

2

THE FAN –
KENNY LYNCH OBE

Kenny Lynch is from London's East End and is a lifelong supporter of West Ham United. I met him in a café in Golders Green in the spring of 1999.

Lynch was one of the relatively few black singers on the British pop scene in the early 1960s, and made the Top Ten a couple of times in 1963 with 'You Can Never Stop Me Loving You' and a cover of the Drifters' 'Up on the Roof'. His records had the feel of American pop-soul, at times sounding a little like the songs being recorded by Gene Pitney and Gene McDaniels during the same era.

'Kipper', as he is know to those close to him, the younger brother of jazz singer Maxine Daniels, has always been central to the mechanism that makes British entertainment tick. He is a living pioneer of British black music traditions and has had several hit singles to his credit, many of which are self-penned gems. Some of his songs have become cult classics, such as 'After All', 'My Own Two Feet' and 'Movin' Away', which have been Northern Soul collectables for years.

Early in 1963, Lynch had been on the same bill as the Beatles on the group's first British tour. In January of that year, John Lennon and Paul McCartney wrote 'Misery', in the hope that the artist with top billing, Helen Shapiro, would record it. Shapiro's producer turned it down, but Lynch took the composition and gave it a much more pop-oriented arrangement than the Beatles would later use when they recorded the song themselves on their debut album *Please Please Me*, which was released just a week after Lynch's version of the song.

A consummate stylist, Kenny has demonstrated his talent as a songwriter with the uptown soul sounds of 'For Loving You, Baby' or 'I'll Stay By You'. Uniquely for a British songwriter, Lynch worked in the Brill Building in New York at a time when that was the creative hub of the Phil Spector sound (amongst others). There, he helped American music to incorporate British sensibility. On 'What Am I To You', Kenny cocked an ear towards Burt Bacharach, and he showed his ability to home in on the very essence of pop with his co-composition 'Sha La La La Lee' for fellow Cockneys the Small Faces. It was to be the band's biggest worldwide hit, and his co-writer was none other than the legendary Mort Schumann, the Brill Building songwriter who had collaborated with Doc Pomus to pen such classics as 'Save the Last Dance for Me' and 'Teenager in Love'. Lynch wrote or co-wrote other songs from the Small Faces' 1966 debut album *You'd Better Believe It* (co-written with American soul writer/producer Jerry Ragavoy) and 'Sorry She's Mine', which could have been strong enough to make it under its own steam had it been released as a single.

His compositions have been recorded by such pop greats as the Drifters, the Swinging Blue Jeans and Cilla Black; a couple of his more notable efforts were the fine girl-group-styled 'He's Got Something' by Dusty Springfield, and a hit by Billy J Kramer, 'It's Gotta Last Forever'.

As well as singing and songwriting, Kenny has performed as a dancer and actor, and has done stand-up comedy and sketches, working in television, radio and film. He has worked in management and production, helping many newcomers into the business.

He has come a long way since first singing with his big sister Maxine in 1950. Kenny appeared very frequently on our TV screens during the 1960s and he was such an all-round entertainer that some people may associate him with various disciplines from that period. Certainly, Kenny was a groundbreaking and creative comedian – although today's 'alternative' comedy may be thought to tackle taboo subjects, Kenny would doubtless claim that he'd done it all years before.

Kenny's view of being part of West Ham United's support up to the time when Clyde Best, Clive Charles and Ade Coker played for the Hammers, gives a unique and historical insight into a bygone footballing era, and offers a real flavour of how dramatic it must have been for three black players to take to the field in the cause of East London's soccer aspirations.

'From the age of about seven, I've gone over to Upton Park. I used to go all on my own and my mother and father weren't worried about me or anything. Now, you couldn't do that. I'm 61 now...

'I was a Stepney lad. In the middle of the war, we moved down to East India Dock Road. I lived where the Commercial Road ends, by the big pub, The Eastern, which became The Londoner. I went to a school called Farant Street, later called the Sir Humphrey Gilbert – they changed the name to make it sound a bit posher, but it was still full of ragamuffins.

'I started in showbusiness about a year after I started going to West Ham. I was singing just up near Rathbone Street; there was a school for dancers called Peggy O'Farrell's Dancers, which is still going, but she's dead, I think. They do all those things like Annie... I went there and I thought I might learn to dance, but I wasn't that good and they said, "Why don't you just sing?" So I used to sing about four numbers during the shows. They used to do them at Stratford Town Hall and Poplar Civic, those sorts of places; I'd just sing and the kids would dance behind me.

'My father was a stoker at Beckton Gas Works; he was a stoker in the Merchant Navy during the war. Mum was busy with seven kids. Originally, there were 11 of us, but some died; my eldest brother got torpedoed in the Navy.

'I'm married to Julie, who's from Barry in Wales, where I met her. My kid, although she's a girl, she's named after Bobby Moore, who was going to be her godfather but he died three weeks before she was born. I was going to call

her Roberta like Bobby's kid, but I thought, Sod it, because he died I was so upset I called her Bobby and she goes round telling everybody in school that she's Bobby Moore.

'Bobby was my best friend all of the time. I had a business with him for about six years before he died. It was called Bobby Moore's World of Soccer. We used to go all round the country with Greavesie or Bestie or other football greats, and I'd be the Michael Parkinson of the evening, asking, "You with the red shirt, what's your question?" We showed a film with 50 great goals, all from different matches and teams.

'Towards the end of Bobby's life, we cancelled some of the gigs because he wasn't well enough to do them. At the time, we were both on this committee to enable children to go to Disneyland. He was supposed to go to Florida with the kids, and he phoned me up and asked me to go as he wasn't feeling too well; he told me to take someone with me, so I took Frank McLintock. I took Peter Cook as well, and he died just after we'd got back.

'I'd just had a bypass myself, having only come out of hospital two weeks before. Bobby and I used to talk to each other all the time, every day; we always talked two or three times a day, and once he phoned me up at eleven o'clock at night and he sounded terrible. For the first time, I didn't recognise his voice. I said, "Who's that?" and he said, "It's Bobby. Who d'yer think it is?" I said I was expecting somebody else, as I didn't want to make him feel worse. I said, "What do you want?" He said, "I'm worried about yer." So I said, "I'm worried about you." "I'll tell you what we'll

do," he says, "you worry about me and I'll worry about you and we'll leave it that way." Then he put the phone down. Six o'clock the next morning, he died.

'Stephanie rang me up, it must have been about nine o'clock in the morning, and I was very upset. I was going off to do the Gloria Hunniford radio show. I rang up the show because I thought I wouldn't be able to do it; I was supposed to make a few quips and that. She had an American producer at the time and I said to him that I wasn't coming; he said that he didn't think I would, saying, "I know about your pal." I asked him how he knew about that and he told me, "We all know, but we're not letting it out until four o'clock." I didn't do anything that day.

'I still go through my drawers and things and find things to do with him. We had a company, and it always jolts me a bit.

'I was a sort of East End celebrity singer in the pubs and all the players from the different teams used to come in and see me. Bobby came into a pub I was in one night and we got to talking and he said, "We go down the Ilford Palais a lot." I said, "I'll come down there one night... what's the best night?" He said Tuesday or Thursday, so I said, "I'll see yer down there," so from then on we were kind of inseparable. We didn't see one another every day, but we stayed together 'til the day he died. I might have been the last person who spoke to him, apart from Steph, I'm not sure.

'Bobby was the best player I ever saw at West Ham. Trevor Brooking was superb, too - he was slow, but I thought he

18

was a great player. Malcolm Allison was a rock for them when I was a kid; I used to love Ernie Gregory because I always wanted to be a goalkeeper.

'From when I was about 16, I used to go into the dressing room after the game; they knew I was a supporter. I met Bobby when I was about 15. I was singing in these pubs but I had to leave at ten o'clock because you weren't allowed to be in a boozer because of the age thing.

'I played twice in charity games at Upton Park, and scored two against Ernie – he was sick as a pig! I played in a Showbiz XI, having fixed it up with Reg Pratt for us to play there a couple of times, but I never thought of taking it up; I was absolutely useless.

'I had seven records in the charts; I listened for two weeks after I finished them before they come out and I never want to hear them again unless I'm miming to them on television or something. My greatest achievement in showbusiness is still being around. If someone had told me when I was a kid that I'd still be around now, I'd have said, "You're crazy!"

'I did two years on tour with the Beatles. I think it's in Trivial Pursuit that I'm the first person ever to record a Beatles song – "Misery". They actually wrote it on the coach for Helen Shapiro, and she said, "I don't think it's really me," and I said, "Oh, I'll do it. I'm doing a session next week... put it on tape and I'll do it." I took it to Walley Ridley my A&R man, and he said, "Yeah, I like it." It was a complete and utter miss!

'During one game I was sitting with one of the injured

19

players, Alan Sealey. They were playing Arsenal in the last game of the season, and it was like a war zone. Both teams were mid-table, but you would have thought they were playing for the FA Cup, League title and the World Cup; they were kicking each other to pieces. When we left the ground, we used to go down to Ilford, to the steak house, with Martin and Geoff and the wives. We'd go there after mid-week games particularly, the seven o'clock games. I was living in Chelsea then, and on Saturdays we used to go straight over to the Black Lion.

'After that Arsenal match, Bobby had all these bumps all over him. Peter Storey was in the Arsenal side at the time. There were some villains in that side. But we had a few that could put it about, like Billy Bonds. The dirtiest people in football are the forwards, though, because they get away with it more.

'I've supported the team all my life and I've got a funny feeling that we want the team the way they are – not particularly successful. It's been nice this year with no relegation fights, but I've got nothing to fight for this year – it's over for them. Last year, I'm thinking, Oh shit, I hope they don't go down. But that's what I like about the club, because when I was originally there it was a small, family club. It had a regular 28,000 dyed-in-the-wool supporters, and nobody thought about sacking the manager; if the team played shit, then we said they played shit. Blimey, it's not the manager's fault. But now, they're still great.

'Me and Bobby went to Upton Park after he'd finished playing; we'd occasionally go to a game, and we used to be

able to park in the directors' car park. On one occasion, there were all those National Front bastards outside. One of them knocked on the window. Bobby was driving, and I was sitting there reading the paper, and this guy was selling Bulldog or whatever it's called. He shouted to Bobby, "What you doing with that black bastard?" I was very choked that that happened at West Ham. I'd never come across that sort of thing before at the club. Mooro was really sick about it. He said, "Piss off!" and put the window up.

'But, apart from that, I think the West Ham crowd are great. I used to know everybody there. When I was a kid, I used to stand on the terraces and later on I was in the directors' box. Reg Pratt, God rest his soul, was a great friend. I used to mix with all the players, telling jokes and that. They were getting £20 a week then; they weren't much better off than the ordinary working man. I can remember Bobby saying to me in the car one day going to West Ham, "I'm the highest-paid footballer in England." I said, "How much you got then on your contract?" And he said, "280 quid," and I said, "Don't tell bloody lies."

'There's guys in the game now getting more in a week than Bobby ever got in his whole life. Eighty grand some of 'em, and they couldn't walk in his shoes.

'When I first went to West Ham, there weren't many black fans. I think me and Charlo [John Charles, West Ham's first black player] were the only ones in the ground. When you're seven years old, you don't even know you're black. There were some black players around – Paul Reaney at Leeds, Charlo at West Ham and Charlie Williams had been

21

at Doncaster. He was another hard bastard. He was a great kicker; kicked everything that moved. He used to leave stud marks on their necks.

'Me and Mooro made a movie over at Upton Park – Till Death Us Do Part. They asked us to do this bit with Alf Garnett in the Black Lion. Mooro could drink like nobody I've ever known and stay straight as a die. We had to drink these two lagers and Alf Garnett would come up and tap him on the shoulder and go, "Oy, Mooro! Our captain... he's got a coon with him..." and all that. I had to call Mooro over and say, "Tell him to piss off." Course, Mooro was doing that and the director kept saying, "Cut, do it again," and we did about 30 takes. The only way you could tell Mooro was pissed was by looking into his eyes; he'd smile and his eyes would go sort of smiley. I can't drink that many lagers – I was taking a sip and topping up – but Mooro was just putting them away and starting again on every take. I used to say he had a hollow leg. After about 15 or 20 takes, I noticed that Mooro was really pissed, so on the next take I said to him, "Tell him to fuck off," and he turned straight round to Alf and said, "Fuck off!" When I think about West Ham, I always think about that day when I made him do that.

'Of course, it was a landmark moment when Clive Charles, Ade Coker and Clyde Best all played in the same team. Bestie was a phenomenon, wasn't he? He was the one everyone knew about. He was such a great big bloke, but could he run! And he had a lot of skill – nice touches. He scored his share of goals, good goals, too. But Clyde did other things as well. He held up play like a great big wall

and, of course, as he was running through carrying two or three defenders with him, he opened up the way for others. He was a fantastic asset. I think he'd have been bigger today than he was then.

'Like most people, I knew more about John Charles as a player than Clive, but I remember him being a really silky defender. I'm not surprised he got on well in the States; they would like the way he did things – bit of style and that. It was a shame for him that there were two or three other good backs at the club at the same time. Again, he wouldn't look out of place playing for a team like Manchester United now, would he? Ten years ahead of his time… or perhaps six.

'Maybe Clive would have been better starting out somewhere like Orient or something and then working his way up. But he's done well for himself so, in the end, it's all to the good.

'Having those three on the park said something about West Ham as a football club, but it also said a lot about the way society was going. It was the start of something good, that's for sure, and look at the talent black lads bring to English football now. It's a bit like the way Motown was breaking ground at around the same time; a whole world of sounds coming from black people. It was just like the football, really… it added just a bit of a different dimension. Yeah, the Hammers broke the mould that day, opened doors. But that is what happened at West Ham; the club has always been innovative. The world has grown up a bit now and good thing, too. But it was a great day. A historic day!'

3

AMERICAN SOCCER – THE GOAL BUSINESS

The primal National American Soccer League (NASL) was impressive in terms of play, but, as the Atlanta Chiefs were winning the first NASL Championship in 1967, it was obvious that financial success continued to evade professional soccer in North America – the crowds didn't come. In its debut season, the league gates were below 4,000 on average; this was not enough to break even. Millions of dollars had been lost, which provoked the owners to insist on assurances that they would get a return on their capital. As it turned out, the lack of a proper base for many teams was certainly a factor in the lack of success. Of course, this was one of the main draws for investors in the first place, that they would have minimal layout on the basic soccer product. However, this also meant that the game didn't really have any concrete assets apart from the players, most of whom were journeymen and/or little more than negative equity in terms of their contracts; most were never going to be 'sold on' and certainly not at a profit when related to the inflated wages some players were receiving.

But the dream still endured that soccer might now fulfil its supposed potential in North America. It was hoped that the public, being freed of the confusion caused by the existence of two leagues, would flock to games and fill the leased and borrowed stadiums. However, this was little more than the wishful thinking of those deluded by their own fancies rather than the solid plan of the detached business brain. In effect, the whole project was amounting to little more than a tactic of sending good money after bad. As such, the season was not old as a frightening number of the clubs found themselves wading in the mire of mounting fiscal problems; more money was going out than was coming in.

However, twice during 1967, the NASL got a significant boost from the great Pelé, who was on a world tour with his club Santos. While even the likes of Bobby Moore and Eusébio were unfamiliar names to Americans, the vast majority of sports fans in the USA and Canada were familiar with Pelé.

Santos began their tour of NASL clubs with a 3-2 defeat of St Louis Stars. This was followed with a 4-1 win over the Kansas City Spurs and a 7-1 massacre of the Boston Beacons. But, in Cleveland, the Stokers beat the mighty Brazilians 2-1. Pelé experienced a second defeat at the hands of the Generals, who achieved a 5-3 victory in New York. But the tourists finished off their schedule on a high note, a 3-1 win against the Washington Whips.

Pelé was eulogised non-stop throughout his stay in North America, and even the usually anti-soccer US media sung his praises. Interest was stirred and gates for league games reflected a new mood about and attitude towards the game. But the seeming renaissance turned out to be an aberration when crowds fell to their 'pre-Pelé' levels after Santos flew south. The *Peixe* (the nickname for Santos, which means, 'the Fish', although the team's traditional mascot is a whale) undertook a subsequent tour later in the season with a similar result. They defeated the eventual NASL Champions, Atlanta Chiefs, 6–2; and the Oakland Clippers, winners of the NPSL title the previous season, were beaten 3–1.

Seven years later, Pelé would bring global attention to the NASL and provide the momentum for its most successful years. But, following the second Santos tour, nearly all the NASL clubs were suffering deep financial problems. The owners began to cut their losses and, one by one, in what looked like domino fashion, clubs folded.

At the start of 1969, 12 of the 17 original NASL sides had disappeared, along with the league's television contract. The ratings for matches were unacceptable even by weekend daytime standards. As such, another season looked highly unlikely. The league office closed, and even the records of the 1967 and 1968 seasons vanished.

However, after the wreckage, individuals emerged who had a continuing belief that soccer had a future in America; one such person was the owner of the Dallas Tornado, Lamar Hunt. Tornado are probably the only club to have completed a world tour before running out for their first home match.

Bob Kap, the Dallas coach, while pulling together a side for the 1968 season, decided to avoid taking on experienced professionals and looked to recruit a tight band of younger players from Britain, Holland and Scandinavia. Trying to build a team ethos, Kap led the resultant inexperienced group on a kind of educational trip, taking in Spain, Morocco, Turkey, Cyprus, Iran, Pakistan, India, Ceylon, Burma, Malaysia, Indonesia, Vietnam, Taiwan, Japan, the Philippines, Australia, New Zealand and Fiji, concluding the tour in Tahiti. Bob's boys contested 45 matches, claimed 10 victories, suffered 27 defeats and drew eight. Throughout their journey, this 'American' club team flew 'Old Glory', although there wasn't a single player in the squad who had even visited the United States.

In Dallas, the team endured a torturous opening run that extended to 21 matches without a win. Over the 32-game NASL schedule, the club claimed just two wins. Predictably, Kap got the sack (headlines in local papers included the predictable but oddly satisfying 'KAP SACK') well before the end of the season. For all this, Lamar Hunt remained focused, alongside Phil Woosnam, the former captain of West Ham United and the coach who had taken the Atlanta Chiefs to the NASL title. Together, they laboured to create a modestly financed organisation that would carry the league into the 1969 season. Woosnam, now the League Commissioner, with Hunt, saw that they had limited prospects in terms of time, so they had every motivation to convince Clive Toye, the former general manager of the Baltimore Bays and English soccer writer, to collaborate with them.

It was on 28 March 1985 that the NASL passed into history. For 19 years, it had been the conduit of the game in the USA and Canada and had fought hard for a place between the great monoliths of American sport – baseball, grid-iron football, basketball and ice hockey – at a time when all these were escalating as industries in the burgeoning US economy.

The NASL had soldiered on through the hard and even harder times at the start of the 1970s, ultimately achieving what appeared to be its objective in the final years of that decade with nearly 70,000 people turning up for matches just outside New York City at Giants Stadium in the Meadowlands; but this was not to last. In the first part of the 1980s, the NASL began a demise that eventually concluded with its being obliged to call a 'suspension of operations' – American managerial speak for 'gone bust'.

However, the NASL had taken soccer in the USA into a new era and had dragged it a long way from the founding of the United Soccer Association. The aptly acronymic USA was inaugurated with the support of the United States Soccer Football Association (USSFA, now the United States Soccer Federation, USSF) and FIFA, although it was not an American league in what might be the common understanding of such a notion, being made up of British and other European sides playing during the summer. Sunderland, Stoke City, Hibernian and Wolverhampton Wanderers became the Cleveland Stokers, Los Angeles Wolves, Toronto City and the Vancouver Royal Canadians, linking the end of one British season with the start of another in what was often quite torrid competition.

The temporary transplantation of clubs from abroad in the baseball and grid-iron football grounds of North America started in earnest with the American International Soccer League (ISL) in 1960. West Ham United played in this tournament and the American Challenge Cup in 1963 against other British, European and South American clubs as 'The Baltimore Bays'.

Founder of this summer carnival of soccer was entrepreneur Bill Cox. The ISL also organised visits of overseas teams that competed under their 'real' titles in tournaments that were played out right across America, and these competitions were well received.

Constant rancour between the USSFA and the exuberant Bill Cox concluded with the end of the ISL following the 1965 tournament. The resultant vacuum cleared the way for a revamped version of the 'tourist' concept that took the form of a short league programme with visiting clubs representing American cities.

However, Bill Cox, with the aid of American sports owners, set up an authentic American First Division. But, not long after this move, Richard Millen and Jack Kent Cooke, both of whom had been involved with Cox's idea to initiate a genuine American soccer product, made efforts to form their own groups to inaugurate a US First Division.

The comparatively anonymous USSFA was the single body with the power to grant official first-division status and only players that were involved in USSFA-recognised leagues were allowed into international competition.

The vision of providing quality professional soccer in the

North American milieu was shared by three distinct groups of entrepreneurs during the first half of 1966. They beset the headquarters of the USSFA (now USSF) and the Canadian Soccer Football Association (CSFA) (that would become the Canadian Soccer Association) which were both taken completely by surprise by the enthusiasm these people had to energise the game in the USA.

Frank Woods, the USSFA president, put together a committee to appraise and choose which bid would be given sanction. However, Cox had been busy putting his league together and organising a timetable to start the following year.

Those prepared to put their money into soccer were encouraged to do so by the appreciable numbers turning up to watch matches in Europe, Africa and South America. There was also a belief that soccer could be repackaged so as to appeal to the American sports-going public and make use of the many huge stadiums that existed across the USA during periods when baseball and grid-iron teams were playing on their competitors' home turf. For those looking to build the professional game in the USA, it seemed obvious that the biggest consideration, the necessary 'plant', was already in place. All that was needed was the personnel and the fan base, the 'soft' resources that could be relatively easily set in place and generated.

The idea of transplanting soccer in the USA was not new; immigration from South America and Europe had always given the game a peripheral place in America, but the 1966 World Cup in England, with English-speaking coverage and a worldwide audience via the BBC, made the whole enterprise of promoting football more appetising for American investors. Right across North America, a new television audience watched a sporting event that, in significance, was second only to the Olympics. The thrilling Wembley Final that pitted England against West Germany (not much more than 20 years after the Second World War), which Americans, thanks to NBC-TV, saw as good as live (the technology of the time meant that there was a slight delay between events happening and the pictures appearing on TV sets in the States), whetted the appetite of the public and grabbed the attention of sports businesspeople.

However, the reaction to this massive, unique event was never going to be a substitute for the rigorous market analysis that never happened before the 'soccer product' came galloping into the gun-slinging atmosphere of the American sporting landscape. The vast majority of Americans and Canadians had been born and brought up with little if any knowledge of the history, culture or even most basic rules of Association Football. At the same time, the interest and enthusiasm generated by the World Cup could not be immediately capitalised on; most people in the United States who watched Bobby Moore lift the Jules Rimet trophy could only build on any interest they might have had by going to buy a season ticket for a local club. Unfortunately, in most places there were no local clubs, and in places where established clubs did exist they were tiny enterprises fostered by a handful of European or South American immigrants on a scale equivalent to a British pub team.

Nevertheless, investors were encouraged by the idea that there was an untapped spectator market, making an 'ethnic fan dollar' a real possibility. This, of course, assumed that these fans were in a financial position, as a group, to support a new brand. However, this apart, the idea that vast legions of, for example, Ukrainian immigrants would readily march off to support the same soccer team as Venezuelans and Italians was somewhat idealistic. But probably more pertinent was the fact that those people living in America who had allegiance to soccer recognised the gap between the soccer clubs they supported from afar, via the passionate mix of identity, nostalgia and loyalty, and what was offered by way of the 'local product'.

True, if Scotland had played Spain, or Celtic had met Barcelona in New York City at almost any time of any day of the week, a healthy crowd would have turned up to watch, but the vast majority would have had Scottish or Spanish roots; the 'ethnic dollar' bought an 'ethnic product'; Hot Dog United v Apple Pie Rovers would not have the same appeal.

This situation was made obvious when the United States and Canadian national teams played; even on their home grounds, most of the crowd was made up of people who had been born in Europe or South America.

However, soccer had captured the belief and imagination of enough investors to override any of the lessons previously learned about transplanting the game in the 'home of the brave' and the great experiment was initiated. But, as is the tradition of enterprise culture in American sport, there was a showdown between the groups that looked to cash in on soccer.

The first shots were fired by the USSFA, who, in collaboration with the CSFA, determined to authorise just one of the three consortia that requested authorisation to create a professional league to operate on a coast-to-coast basis. The option of having a number of competing leagues, fighting between one another for what support there was, would not have served the game well and, anyway, there was a sort of unvoiced agreement that North America would not be able to support more than one professional league.

However, sanctions have never stopped American capitalists. The national associations in the United States and Canada required each club accepted into their framework to pay a hefty $25,000 franchise fee, 4 per cent of what their fans paid to watch live games and 10 per cent of the television revenue. The NASL settled for this arrangement, but Cox rejected the USSFA's terms, so official backing went to Jack Kent Cooke, the owner of the Washington Redskins, and his United Soccer Association, that received the Division One status.

The idea was that Cooke's USA would play host to foreign clubs while developing home-grown sides that, in time, would replace the imported teams. It was envisaged that, over a two-year period, a European club-type structure would come into being in the North America context.

But Cox was not to be beaten. He combined his resources with Richard Millen's National Soccer League (the other defeated bid) to create the National Professional Soccer League (NPSL), then filed a suit against FIFA, the USSFA and the Canadian authorities for pronouncing them to be an outlaw body, and started to lay plans to field teams. However, the important realisation on the parts of both Cox and Millen was that an authentic North American league could not be made up of imported sides. With this driving ethic, they determined to commence their league in 1967 with ten new teams.

For all this, NPSL teams and players were barred from having any dealings with organisations or clubs that the national associations had sanctioned; this included global concerns like FIFA and any associations or clubs affiliated to such bodies.

So, during the spring of 1967, there were two professional soccer leagues operating in the United States and Canada. The USA, who some called 'The Inlaws', made the decision to import whole club teams to represent the 12 cities it operated in. The NPSL, sometimes known as 'The Outlaws', populated its ten clubs with players enlisted from all over the world.

Unlike its rival, the NPSL had acquired a national television contract with CBS which was renewable yearly. This made provision for a game of the week, with minimal advertising revenue returning to the league; this got the outlawed NPSL started and it kicked off with the Baltimore Bays playing at home to the Atlanta Chiefs on 16 April. The match was televised live. Jack Whittaker, one of the network's top sports commentators, covered the game with the help of Danny Blanchflower, the ex-Northern Ireland international captain. Danny, by this time a seasoned media man, described the matches in a frank and honest manner and made no attempt to hide his generally low opinion of the standard of play. One such comment that stands out in my memory was his likening a hapless goalkeeper to 'a lunatic bog toad with a nervous twitch'. At another point, observing a chaotic game in which the players seemed to not have an inkling of what they were doing or why, he asked if the cameras had turned up at the 'Ballytown spinster's hoedown' by mistake. Such bluntness was (and probably still would be) anathema to North American audiences that are not used to frank criticism, particularly delivered via swingeing metaphor, in sports coverage; club owners were certainly surprised to hear their 'products' heartily condemned on national television with devastatingly pithy assessments such as 'useless', 'laughable' and 'tragically naive'. For them, it was akin to paying for a commercial that told the world that their merchandise was garbage.

A further difficulty during that initial season of televising the NPSL was how and where to slot advertisements into the game. The traditional American sports – baseball, football and ice hockey – include breaks in the action that are perfect for fitting in television commercials. Soccer is not so accommodating. This being the case, the television tsars decided to arrange their own breaks... with the support of the referee. Just four weeks into the season, it was revealed that 11 of the 21 free-kicks given by referee Peter Rhodes in the match between Toronto and Pittsburgh were awarded in 'co-operation' with CBS, to facilitate commercials!

The United Soccer Association began play two weeks later. Although average attendances for NPSL matches had been hovering around the 5,000 mark, in their first few weeks of operation, the USA did better. For instance, 34,965 came to the Houston Astrodome to watch the encounter between Houston Stars and the Los Angeles Wolves. It seemed that the USA modus operandi of effectively leasing teams was working.

But, when the season concluded, it was clear that crowds for both leagues had fallen very short of what the owners had expected and planned for. Indeed, the figures were poor enough to provoke alarm. Both leagues could attract good crowds and a few matches drew around the 30,000 mark, although the average over all games was fewer than 10,000 per match.

As the first season came to a close, it was clear that the audience for North American soccer could not support two professional leagues and, holding on to their television contract, the rival leagues combined.

Necessity had dictated that the tactic of survival of the fittest had to be dropped (neither league was very fit) and the cause to make soccer happen in America had to take precedence. It took months of negotiation but, in the end, the merger agreement was signed just prior to Christmas 1967 and the 17-club North American Soccer League was born.

The success of soccer in the States was dependent on fans becoming enamoured with the game, and having the opportunity of seeing the greatest exponents of it and the world's best clubs, all displaying their skills on US turf. West Ham, among others at the time, were instrumental in bringing the best of British to the American public, and helped to kick-start the game's toe-hold in many ways.

In the summer of 1963, having completed their international duties, Johnny Byrne and Bobby Moore joined their West Ham team-mates who were part-way through the ISL tournament. Fourteen teams took part in two groups. The Irons played their group games in New York, Chicago and Detroit. By the time Budgie and Mooro got to the States, the Hammers had played two games, managing just a single point, and were bottom of their league, which included sides from Scotland, Italy, France, West Germany, Mexico and Brazil. Within less than a day of breathing American air, Byrne and Moore found themselves playing in a West Ham XI a goal down at half-time to the Mexican side Oro at New York's Randalls Island Stadium, which usually hosted baseball games. The second 45 minutes started fast and furious, and, with Moore marshalling his team at the heart of defence, the Hammers were a different side to the one that started the tournament and it was a long pass from Moore that turned the game. Byrne killed the ball on his chest, turning himself and the ball as he did so and darted into the box. The Mexican defenders flew at him one after the other and it was the third tackle that cut him down; it was a clear penalty. Byrne put the East Londoners level from the spot, and he then made the next two goals for Geoff Hurst and the Hammers got their first win of the tournament.

However, a sterner test awaited the Irons. In the powerful glow of Detroit's University Stadium floodlights, Preussen Munster of West Germany and 10,000 or so of Detroit's massive German–American community were their opponents in a match that was billed as a contest between

38

England and Germany. Preussen were a dour, stoic, stolid side, built on the bedrock of precision and discipline. They were a redoubtable unit of Teutonic knights, without fear or compassion, and for 70 minutes they met West Ham's urbane football aesthetic with grim and focused athleticism set within an iron wall of defensive sobriety. It was a Moore-to-Byrne move that led to Hurst breaking the deadlock with 20 minutes of the game left. Martin Peters got West Ham's second following a sweet one-two with Byrne that totally wrong-footed the bedazzled German defence.

The next trial was an evening match in New York where West Ham faced Valenciennes, a side that were the very antithesis of Munster. It was an evening match and the temperature was over 35°C in New York. A Hurst hat-trick made West Ham look invincible.

The Hammers now needed just one point in their last game against the Brazilians, Recife, to give them the Championship. But the hellishly hot conditions of the Randalls Island pitch suited the boys from Brazil much more than it did the Boleyn Ground lads. For all that, West Ham went into the break one-up by way of a Johnny Byrne combination with Martin Peters and a drive from ten yards out.

But, five minutes into the second half, Jose Matos brought his side back into the game. With the heat taking its toll, West Ham had to work hard to gain the necessary draw. This was all the more impressive given that Alan Sealey had been sent off during the game, seemingly for allowing himself to be kicked to the ground by the Brazilians. He was treated for his injuries before the referee ordered him to leave the field of play.

West Ham came back to England as 'International Soccer League Champions', but this had qualified them for the American Challenge Cup (ACC), so, after just a few weeks back home, the Hammers were again making a return journey across the Atlantic.

The ACC tournament consisted of two ties. In the first, West Ham would play the tough Poles of Gornik who had won another league that had been played out at the same time as the Hammers had been contesting the ISL Championship. The second game, which would decide the destination of the Cup, would be between the winners of the Gornik–West Ham match and the American Challenge Cup winners of the previous year. The Gornik side were tough and skilful. They had defeated Spurs 4–2 in their home leg of the European Cup and included a future World Cup player, Lubanski, in their starting XI.

The first of the two games against Gornik was staged at Randalls Island. In the first midweek match, a floodlit event that took place in front of the relatively big crowd of 10,000, West Ham were always faster and more intelligent than their opponents. Byrne scored the vital goal that gave West Ham a 1–1 draw. It came from a really juicy drive, hit from a central position just inside the box.

The second match against Gornik was contested on a steamy Sunday afternoon. Geoff Hurst's first-half goal (his ninth of the tournament) was created out of nothing by Byrne. Two disallowed Gornik goals in the second 45 minutes caused tempers among the watching Poles to boil over. A pitch invasion caused injury to the referee and a hold-up of

30 minutes that almost became the prelude to the abandonment of the match. But the game was finally concluded and West Ham made for Chicago and the first leg of the Final against Dukla of Czechoslovakia, who were looking for a hat-trick of American Challenge Cup wins.

The men from Prague came to the 'Windy City' with Josef Masopust, European Footballer of the Year in 1962, and Svatopluk Pluskal, who had turned out in all six of his country's World Cup games in Chile. Indeed, more than half of the Czech national side that had played in that World Cup were in the Dukla ranks. However, under the dazzling floodlights in the huge 110,000-seat Soldier Field, in which the 11,000 crowd looked lost, the tough Czechs seemed intimidated by the West Ham side, enough to retreat into defence after scoring the only goal of the first leg.

In the second leg on the following Sunday afternoon, which was played back at Randalls Island before a crowd of 15,000, the largest of the tournament, it took a fantastic display by Czech international goalkeeper Pavel Kouba to keep Hurst, liberally supplied by the feet of Byrne, from netting a hatful. But claret-and-blue pressure told when Tony Scott put West Ham ahead. Then, against the run of play, 59-cap Josef Masopust's goal caused Dukla to avoid defeat and retain the Cup.

West Ham's American expeditions had provided a marvellous experience for the young Irons, whose average age was just 23. They had given the seasoned Czechs a close run and had matched some of the strongest club teams in the world. Geoff Hurst came back to England as the tournament's top scorer with nine goals and Bobby Moore was awarded the 'Eisenhower Trophy' as the Player of the Series.

Later, Ron Greenwood was to declare, 'Our second game against Dukla was the most perfect technical display I have seen from any British team I have been connected with... The team gained more experience in ten matches against teams from other nations than the average League player at home gains in 15 years. We learned more that summer about how the game was evolving around the world than we would have done in five European campaigns.'

The Hammers had seen how well they could play as a unit and match teams and players that would have tested the very best of British sides. They had, perhaps, come of age in America.

West Ham returned to America in the summer of 1965, having won the FA Cup the previous season and three weeks after their European Cup Winners' Cup triumph at Wembley. The Hammers were again taking part in the New York International Tournament, but they got off to a poor start against an 'all-star' side entitled 'New Yorkers', losing 2–1 at Randalls Island. The Irons then met Munich 1860 in a repeat of the Cup Winners' Cup Final, and beat the Germans 2–1. Peters and Sealey scored against a half-strength Munich side.

After the defeat of Munich, the Irons met Portuguesa in the Shea Stadium, which had never before been used for soccer. It was a tremendous arena that is famed in the history of music for hosting a legendary Beatles concert, but the venue outshone the game; West Ham lost 6–3. The scoreline flattered the Brazilians; the Hammers squandered a string of chances, but it really was a case of South American football beating the British brand.

In the next game, West Ham were beaten again by New Yorkers, but this time the score was 3-1. Games against the Italians, Varese, and another match against Portuguesa followed. The East Londoners could not qualify, whatever they did, so these encounters became no more than practice matches. All in all, the tour was something of a flop as far as the Irons were concerned. West Ham looked a shadow of the team that had done so well in the USA in the summer of 1963. The side were clearly exhausted; the energy, urgency and enthusiasm were simply not there.

Greenwood called his team's performances 'disgraceful', but added, 'Still, the beatings we have taken over here should have cut us down to size. After this, we will not start the new season with any pre-conceived notions of our own greatness, and that is a good thing.'

4

ADE COKER

'We were playing a reserve game and this Ade Coker was playing. Me, Johnny Cushley and Deary [Brian Dear] were playing I remember. Anyway, Ade was useless... he never done a thing. At half-time, he's holding his stomach and he's talking to Robby Jenkins [West Ham's physiotherapist] and Rob asked him, "What's the matter, Ade?" And he went, "I got de ... stom ... och ... up ... sets!"'

JOHN CHARLES – WEST HAM UNITED

'We had great hopes of Ade. He was a very good little player, and probably would have broken through at some point. But we had a lot of good strikers at West Ham at that time and, as things turned out, he had a good career in the United States, playing alongside the likes of Mike Bailey, Willie Morgan and Charlie George, as well as all the excellent foreign players.

'Yes, Ade Coker, I think was one of the first, if not the first African player, apart from South Africans, to play in the First Division. In many ways, of course, he paved the way for others and the African influence on the game in England has been terrific.'

RON GREENWOOD – WEST HAM UNITED AND ENGLAND

'Ade was very talented, a lot of natural ability. It was a shame he was about at the time he was, because we had the likes of Geoff Hurst, Pop Robson and Clyde Best. The other roles he might have worked into were taken up by people like Pat Holland and Trevor Brooking, so it was not going to work for him in the short term at West Ham. It was a shame to see him go, but he did well in the States.

'Could he have made it in England? I think so. But he needed a club like Fulham to come in; a London club would have been good. He went to Lincoln and I think there was some interest from Norwich, but in those days it would have been hard for him to fit in those places. It was hard enough in London. America was probably the right thing for Ade then – he was a lovely boy. Everyone liked him.'

JOHN LYALL – WEST HAM UNITED

It was West Ham's legendary ace scout Wally St Pier who first alerted Ron Greenwood to the bubbly forward Ade Coker. The young Nigerian, born on 19 May 1954 in Lagos, had arrived in London from his homeland aged 11, and found

46

himself playing for the Henry Compton School, which had a strong tradition of fostering footballing talent. Other clubs were taking an interest in the skilful 14-year-old but it was Wally, the man who discovered so many of the great Hammers players from the early 1960s onwards, who spoke to Ade's parents about him joining the Hammers.

His report to manager Ron Greenwood stated that 'the boy is not big, but his close control of the ball looks exceptional, both when dribbling and while running. He has fast reactions and shows that he keeps his mind on who is around him. Good balance, works hard.'

Ade Coker, who knew little more about West Ham than any other professional club, lived in Fulham and had visited Craven Cottage. He could have signed for the West Londoners but chose to start his professional career at Upton Park, having some idea that it was seen as a good place for young players to start a career. He made his debut on 30 October 1971 in the First Division (then the top echelon of the English game) at Selhurst Park. A late injury to Geoff Hurst brought Ade into the reckoning at almost the last minute. He was as surprised as anyone at his inclusion in the first team and it seems he was the last to be told, just half-an-hour before kick-off, that he was to be in the starting XI.

As West Ham's first black player, John Charles told me Ade was prone to a nervous stomach before games, so perhaps it was for the best that he found out about his first senior match for the Irons so late in the day. Sir Geoff Hurst recalled Ade's reaction, saying, 'He looked as if he'd seen a ghost. He sat there in disbelief for about ten minutes with his eyes wide open and aghast.'

At that point, West Ham were in a healthy if undramatic ninth position in the First Division. Crystal Palace were struggling in 21st place, but 41,540 people had turned up to see the London derby. The East Enders' skipper that day, Bobby Moore, told me years later about the anxious young man facing the massive and partisan crowd. 'It's always hard, that first time. No one really goes out without being a bit scared. You want to do well. I felt for Ade, though. He seemed terrified. I had a word with him, told him just to concentrate and that we were all going to help him through it. But he was OK. After his first touch, he played well. Your mind goes on what you're doing after the initial fright. But going out, he didn't know that... no one does until you have to do it.'

For the majority of the West Ham fans at that game (and watching the highlights on the television the next day), it was the first time they had ever heard of Ade Coker. The slight, sinewy, diminutive striker looked anything but a replacement for the strapping figure of Hurst. But Ade made the most of his opportunity, mesmerising the Palace defence with a dazzling display of dribbling and possessional skills.

John Lyall, the Hammers coach and Greenwood's right-hand man at Upton Park in the early 1970s, told me, 'Ade showed a great deal of promise. The game with Palace was the opportunity to try him out and see how he coped. He had looked the part in training and playing games outside the first team; a bit on the small side, of course, but he could jump and had a sense of timing that is so important in football, particularly for a forward.'

Ade's debut for the Irons took place on a bright day, one of those afternoons that make you feel that winter has had a day off and spring has stood in for a bit. This feeling was heightened when the Hammers took the field in what was then called their 'changed kit' of sky-blue shirts with the two claret hoops – their normal claret-and-blue shirts were too much like the Palace colours. With just six minutes played, the Glaziers – ex-Hammer Malcolm Allison would give Palace the epithet of the 'Eagles' years later in homage to Benfica, the 'Eagles of Lisbon' – were unable to deal with a corner slung in by Harry Redknapp, but Ade could; he lashed a left-foot volley into the top corner of the Palace net, giving John Jackson, an exceptionally talented goalkeeper, no chance.

Ade's nifty footwork in that game dominated the attention of both sets of claret-and-blue supporters, of whom I was one. I saw Ade perform the 'stop the ball, spin 180°, take it with you' move that has, in recent years, so often been attributed as Joe Cole's original trademark. Well, Ade Coker did it long before little boy blue Joe!

In fact, according to Ron Greenwood, 'Johnny Byrne used to do that very well and I thought that it was something Ade could take to. He actually didn't need a great deal of practice once we had shown him what we wanted. He just said, "Oh yes," and perfected the move after the second or third try. But there are limits as to how much you can teach that sort of thing. Ade had it in him already; it wasn't actually new to him. A lot of things he did were like that. We were just giving them a name or pulling them out as individual skill points. Up to then they were something that he was doing but just wasn't aware of – they were all taking place in the stream of his play.

'So often, with players like that, you are just ordering things. People like Bobby [Moore] and Trevor [Brooking] were "made" players to some extent; that's not saying they lacked ability but they developed what they had by practice and hard work. Geoff Hurst was the same. Everyone gets better with practice, though, and it is that hard work that makes the difference. Look how long the careers of Geoff, Bobby and Trevor were.'

A headed effort from Billy Bonds in the 14th minute and a third goal 20 minutes into the second half from Clyde Best, who took Ade under his wing while the lad was at Upton Park, gave West Ham a 3–0 win.

The next day, the back pages of the tabloids were plastered with banners such as 'HAMMERS FIND NEW 17-YEAR-OLD STRIKER', 'COKER'S CRACKER' and 'EE-AYE-ADE-O'. The subsequent reports on the game were almost unanimous in proclaiming that Ade was a star of the future. Later, Brian Moore on ITV's *Match of the Day* did his usual straight-man act to Jimmy Hill's chin as the former Fulham fulcrum foamed fanatically over Ade's cracking carnival of a performance. Moore, who commentated on the match, looked back on the game some years later, saying, 'You couldn't help but be impressed by Ade. He fitted the West Ham style so well that day. When West Ham played that way, they looked the most exciting team around. The conditions were perfect for that West Ham team and, of course, Ade shone because the way his team were organised suited him. It was one of those times for West Ham when everything came together. They looked unbeatable when that happened.'

However, the long English winter, the pounding tackling and the relatively poor pitches of the time stymied the young man's creative prowess and Ade was not able to replicate that first stunning performance. He didn't make the first team for West Ham's next scheduled match at their Boleyn Ground home, which ended in a 2-1 defeat at the hands of Sheffield United. He was involved in four more League matches that term. He retained his place following a 1-0 defeat at Huddersfield on 13 November, only to be substituted at Upton Park as Manchester City walked away 2-0 winners.

But it was on 1 April 1972 that Ade contributed to a historic milestone in the chronicles of West Ham United and the development of the English game, when the Irons ran out on to the Upton Park pitch to face Spurs; the West Ham XI included Ade, Best and left-back Clive Charles. It was the first time that three black players had turned out for an English team in the top league of the game. Charles recalled, 'Do you know, I'm not even sure we noticed it. Looking back, you think you must have done, but I certainly don't remember thinking, Oh! There are three black blokes in our team. It was never really like that. To be honest, I was just glad that I was playing and trying to make sure I did a good enough job to keep my place. It was only my second game of the season. Turned out that I didn't get in the next game; Frank Lampard came back. But I did get a place in the last two games of the season. We lost at Highbury but beat Southampton at Upton Park.

'Of course, it was great what happened against Tottenham and, yes, I'm glad I was part of it. And best of all, we beat them!'

Trevor Brooking, the newly elected 'Hammer of the Year', put his side into the lead (against the run of play) with one of the best goals scored at Upton Park that season. He befuddled defender Peter Collins, giving himself the opportunity to curl in a lob from 20 yards out. But the icing on the cake for Ade was the second goal of the game that sealed a 2–0 defeat for the Irons' deadly London rivals. Ade was waiting at the far post for Kevin Lock's cross from the left wing.

Many years later, Ade recalled that he had understood the importance of that spring day in 1972 and how it would have impacted on young black players in Britain. He was to recall it motivating a feeling that there might be opportunities for young men of colour to break into big-time football. However, it is also telling that he saw West Ham as the one club where an occasion of such consequence could take place. For Ade, Upton Park under the sway of Ron Greenwood was a place that looked to, and shaped, the future, seeing skin colour as having no bearing on the endeavour to unearth skill and promise.

It seemed the initial 'Coker fever' was justified when Ade netted twice in half-a-dozen games and he looked well placed to step into Geoff Hurst's striking boots when the World Cup hero joined Stoke City in the summer of 1972. The little African started the first four encounters of the 1972/73 League crusade, and grabbed his third goal for the

Irons' first team in the third game of the season, a 5–2 crushing of Leicester City in the East End. However, in the fifth match of the campaign, Ron Greenwood drafted in Pat Holland as a supplier from the right for Bryan 'Pop' Robson and Clyde Best to produce an intimidating attacking force.

Ade was still in touching distance of inclusion in West Ham's plans at the beginning of the 1973/74 season, but the arrival of the expensive Ted McDougall seemed to seal Ade's fate in the Docklands, although in September 1973 he made double figures in League appearances in a draw with Leicester at Upton Park.

Ade's last run-out as a Hammer was in a 1–1 draw at home to Hereford in the FA Cup on 5 January 1974. This was also Bobby Moore's swansong game for West Ham. The Hammers were disgraced in the replay, going down 2–1 to Hereford, who played their League football two divisions below West Ham and the rest of England's elite teams.

In all, Ade's 11 games as a Hammer yielded only three goals, and that just could not compete with the other striking options at Greenwood's disposal at the time. Ade was a stylish and talented player, a balanced and instinctive poacher in the Jimmy Greaves mould, but there was no room or time for him to flourish at Upton Park in the helter-skelter 1970s, and he would have needed to oust the likes of Best and Robson, clearly too much of an ask for a teenager. According to John Lyall, 'Ade was up against some good and experienced forwards at that time, proven goalscorers, and, between Pop, Bobby Gould and Clyde, all the options were covered. West Ham also had Ted McDougall, who had to be given a chance given the money that was paid for him and he had scored goals at other clubs.'

Looking back, Ade recalls the disappointment of not really breaking through at Upton Park but perfectly understood that he was competing with a mature, proven world-class striker in Geoff Hurst and, following Hurst's departure, he was up against the prolific and experienced Bryan Robson – taking his place was never going to be an option. Ron Greenwood told Ade his approach to younger players was one based on the slow development of their skills. Ade respected his manager's attitude, but began to see himself as the perennial substitute rather than an instant first choice.

Ade had a month on loan with Lincoln City, and retrospectively saw that as another phase in his continuing education, working with and learning from England manager-to-be Graham Taylor.

Starting his gradual departure from Upton Park, Ade played in the North American Soccer League during the summer of 1974. The NASL was growing apace, attracting hordes of players from South America and Europe, and it was a context where Ade was practically guaranteed a place in starting XIs. Then, what began as a stop-gap opportunity became a permanent move when the NASL made him an offer he couldn't refuse.

Ade was sad to turn his back on West Ham but, at the same time, 'pro-soccer' in the USA was an exciting prospect for the young man and he was never to regret his decision to become a pioneer of the modern game in the USA, where he became a star of the mid-1970s, turning out for the Boston

Minutemen between 1974 and 1976. His positive and skilful play appealed to the swashbuckling nature of Bostonians and, with his high energy and constant good humour, he was a popular part of the colourful 'soccer scene' of that era.

In Boston, Ade played and trained alongside former Hammer Alan Wooler for a time and, together, they brought more than a hint of the Boleyn Ground ethos to the Minutemen's play. His other team-mates included Portuguese and Benfica superstars Antonio Simoes and the legendary Eusébio. Ade got on well with both these legends of the game. It was Eusébio who compared Ade to the Hungarian striking genius Péter Palotás, and introduced him to Pelé who saw something of the Brazilian balance and adventure in his game.

Boston had been involved in soccer and the NASL for seven years before the arrival of Coker in the first season of the Minutemen's existence. Boston Rovers (who were, in reality, Ireland's Shamrock Rovers) had operated during 1967 in the United Soccer Association Eastern Division, before changing their name to Boston Beacons the following year.

Boston returned to the NASL to win the Northern Division in 1974 and 1975, with John Coyne and Ade among the leading scorers in the league. The team played some quality football, none much better than an impressive 4–0 rout of the Philadelphia Atoms in 1975. As a 20-year-old, I attended that game and, although the Atoms were not the best side I've seen, Boston put in a performance that was fresh and exciting, providing the kind of game that promised much for the future of the game in America.

1975 was a good season for Ade; he played 15 games for Boston, scored 10 goals and was responsible for six assists. Despite this, the Minutemen plummeted to last place in 1976, and fans deserted them. The team had attracted average crowds of more than 9,000 during their first year, but in successive years this fell to 4,400 and 2,500 respectively.

After 1976, the Boston franchise went out of business. But, despite the Minutemen's career being brief, they performed admirably, and they brought a certain amount of pride to their home grounds – Alumni Stadium in Chestnut Hill, Schaefer Stadium in Foxborough and Veterans Memorial Stadium in Quincy. On a good night, those venues generated a good feeling, one that was very different to, say, Upton Park, but, given a winning performance, they were the background to some good nights out.

Jimmy Johnstone, who played for San José Earthquakes in 1975, remembered Ade as 'a good wee forward… the crowds liked him because he was busy, always looked like he was going to do something. He gave the impression of being interested all the time. He had some nice touches but he wasn't afraid to get back and defend. That's what appealed to the crowds in the States. It has to be all action and Ade looked the part. I think he enjoyed his football, too. That always comes across and is infectious. He was one of those players who, at the end of the game, looked like he didn't want the match to finish. He had a lot to give.'

From 1976 to 1978, Coker was with the Minnesota Kicks. Mike Bailey, formerly of Charlton and Wolves, was also with the Kicks at the time. The team had been formed in 1976 when the NASL side Denver Dynamos relocated to Minnesota and very astutely changed their name. The team spent six years in the NASL, playing 174 regular season games and finishing with a record of 104 wins and 70 defeats; they scored 352 goals while conceding 273. The Kicks claimed 208 points in their career, with a winning percentage of 59.7 per cent.

The Kicks were an outdoor team in the NASL, playing their home games at the Metropolitan Stadium in Bloomington, Minnesota. The atmosphere was a sort of cross between what you might find in a good Scandinavian match and what might be experienced at a baseball game – a kind of affable exuberance and a sense of humour prevailed. During their six years, the Kicks drew an average crowd of 24,381. Minnesota's best attendance was 32,775 in 1977; the lowest gate was 16,605 in 1981.

Minnesota also turned out for 30 regular season games in two seasons in the Indoor League from 1979 to 1981, claiming 20 wins while losing 10 times. Indoors, they scored 168 goals and let in 125, with a winning percentage of 66.7 per cent.

The Kicks folded following the conclusion of the 1981 season, although soccer made a single season return in 1984 when the Fort Lauderdale Strikers transferred to Minnesota, and were renamed the Minnesota Strikers, before moving to the Major Indoor Soccer League (MISL) after the 1984 season.

Stars for the Kicks included US Soccer Hall of Famers Patrick 'Ace' Ntsoelengoe and Alan Willey, the fifth and third league all-time leading scorers respectively. Ron Futcher, who played for several English clubs, including 120 games for Luton Town, scoring 40 goals, and Manchester City, along with Willey played all six Kicks seasons. Ron went on to become the league's fourth all-time leading scorer, provoking the legend 'No one can face the Futcher alone'.

The Minnesota Kicks are remembered for filling the Metropolitan Stadium car park with partying supporters (a celebratory style known as 'tailgating' in the States). It became a cultural phenomenon in the late 1970s, with thousands of fans arriving early to socialise, drink beer and consume beverages from the backs of their cars. You have to have gone to one of these ad hoc events to really understand what it's like, but a cross between a mass barbecue and a car-boot sale goes some way to describing it.

Ade moved on to the San Diego Sockers for the 1978 and 1979 seasons. They had a decent enough record, but would prove to be very much a 'nearly' team in their outdoor incarnation. While there, Ade's career was also nearly curtailed prematurely in 1978 when an untimely tackle resulted in the tearing of anterior and posterior cruciate ligaments. A knee was severely messed up to the extent that the bones were exposed immediately after the incident. A couple of days later, there seemed to be more prospect of amputation below the knee than hope that Ade would return to the professional ranks.

However, after 14 months of treatment, therapy and dogged determination on Ade's part, he returned to football with more enthusiasm than ever. This tale of the overcoming of adversity climaxed with his selection for the American national team. Ade represented the USA half-a-dozen times during the World Cup qualifying rounds of 1986. after defeating the Netherlands Antilles in the Confederation of North, Central American and Caribbean Association Football (CONCACAF) first round, the side finished runners-up in their second-round qualifying group behind Costa Rica and in front of 2006 qualifiers Trinidad and Tobago.

George Best, who played for Los Angeles Aztecs (1976–78), Fort Lauderdale Strikers (1978–79) and San José Earthquakes (1980–81), knew, like most people involved in the NASL, of Ade's fight to regain fitness. 'It was a remarkable feat in itself. The recovery alone was startling, but to come back and play for the USA was a massive act of will on his part. I saw him play, of course, both before and after the injury and, as far as I could tell, he hadn't lost much. He was a strong player and showed what can be done if you keep yourself fit and have determination. With an injury like that, getting over it is 50 per cent about your head, but that's a big 50 per cent, convincing yourself that the whole thing won't stop you. Makes you wonder about the players today, though, doesn't it? Just goes to show how much of the game is in your mind.'

Coker was with Rochester Lancers in 1980 but he rejoined San Diego Sockers in 1982, a team that had started out as the Baltimore Comets in 1974, moved to San Diego as the Jaws in 1976, but, following a one-year stay in Las Vegas, returned as the San Diego Sockers in 1978. Ade was a consistent striker and, while making many goals in his first few years, he wasn't really back on target himself until 1982, when his experience and skill came together to make an impact as one of the leading goal-getters in the NASL. His tally for the season stood at 13 goals and nine assists.

Ade left the Sockers at the end of his NASL career in 1984 on a high, making his final mark in the scoring charts with 16 goals and seven assists. During his time with San Diego, Ade played in the same XI as Kazimierz Denya, the great Polish international, and another former Boleyn Boy, Yilmaz Orhan. Yilmaz and Ade formed a formidable strike-force, making good use of the lessons they had shared at Upton Park. Later, the Frank McAvennie/Tony Cottee era at the Boleyn Ground reminded me of this pairing.

Ade became one of the most feared goalscorers in North America and this caused him to be rated among the top 20 US all-time players by the influential *Sports Illustrated*. His 74 goals and 38 assists in 156 games during his decade in the North American Soccer League places him 15th among the highest all-time scorers in the NASL. To put this achievement into context, George Best is in 23rd spot with 54 goals from 120 matches while, with 55 goals in 177 outings, Ade's erstwhile mentor at Upton Park, Clyde Best, is in 36th place.

A full analysis of Ade's whole time in America provides even more impressive figures:

NASL REGULAR SEASON AND PLAYOFFS

	Regular Season			Playoffs		
	GP	G	A	GP	G	A
1974 Boston Minutemen	18	7	2	2	0	1
1975 Boston Minutemen	15	10	6	1	0	0
1976 Boston Minutemen	14	4	3	-	-	-
1976 Minnesota Kicks	29	0	5	-	-	-
1977 Minnesota Kicks	3	4	2	3	3	0
1978 Minnesota Kicks	3	0	1	-	-	-
1978 San Diego Sockers	5	4	0	-	-	-
1979 San Diego Sockers	8	3	1	6	3	3
1980 Rochester Lancers	6	0	0	-	-	-
1982 San Diego Sockers	20	13	9	4	4	1
1983 San Diego Sockers	20	6	4	-	-	-
1984 San Diego Sockers	22	16	7	1	0	0
Total	**163**	**67**	**40**	**17**	**10**	**5**

GP = Games Played   G = Goals   A = Assists

Ade also distinguished himself in the Major Indoor Soccer Leagues. He ran out for the New York Arrows (1980), Baltimore Blast (1981–82), San Diego Sockers (1983–87) and St Louis Steamers (1987–88).

Ade retired from playing in 1988 and now works at Home Depot, the biggest home-improvement organisation in America. He lives in Seattle in Washington DC with his wife Debbie and two children, Nickolas and Alanna, who have had the benefit of their dad's soccer experience and know-how.

Four-times England international Keith Weller, a fantastically exciting and gifted striker, who played for the New England Tea Men (1978–80) and Fort Lauderdale Strikers (1980–83) after a career in England with Millwall, Chelsea and Leicester City, once said of Ade, 'He does what a good pro would do – gives everything for the team he's playing for. He's clever and became smart to the game in America. If you could have counted the free-kicks and penalties he won, it might be surprising. Yeah, he could have made it in England with the right breaks, but he did OK in the States I think. He was one of the best forwards in the NASL, and that's not bad, is it?'

One of Ade's abiding wishes is that he might return to watch a game at the Boleyn Ground after he retires. He remembers West Ham, like many former players, as a sort of family, which nurtured and cared about him. He recalled the kindness, approachability and encouragement of Bobby Moore, and how the England skipper took time to introduce him to the culture and day-to-day workings of Upton Park. For Ade, West Ham was literally the place that enabled him to 'live the dream' from a very early point in his life, and he was able to see his presence there as preparing the way for other young black men to enrich themselves and make a positive impact first on English and then on European football. In his own words, he felt 'blessed' to have been given a chance to be part of the continued evolution of the game. He kept in contact with Clive Charles, one of his compatriots on 1 April 1972, until the untimely passing of the former Hammer.

As a young player, Coker was perhaps a little too lightweight to take punishment from the likes of Ron Harris and Norman Hunter. John Charles laughed as he told me,

'When someone got within a yard of him, he would go down as if he'd been hit by a train. It took him time to get his timing right, but he could do a bit; a tidy little player.'

But Ade became one of the great players in the mid-20th-century development of the game in North America, playing against and being rated alongside the likes of the brilliant Peruvian international Teofilo Cubillas and Giorgio Chinaglia, who, although born in Carrara, Tuscany, grew up in Wales and started his career with his local club Swansea City. Later, he played for Massese, Internapoli and Lazio in his native Italy where he played for seven seasons. In 1974, Chinaglia led Lazio to the club's first Championship in its history and was the leading scorer in Serie A.

The impact of these world greats, and others, on the evolution of the game in the States was extraordinary, and four in particular – an Italian, a Peruvian and a couple of dyed-in-the-wool Hammers – bear closer examination.

THE ITALIAN DRUID

Chinaglia played 14 times for Italy and scored four goals in the process. He was part of the Italian team that travelled to the 1974 World Cup in West Germany.

Chinaglia joined the NASL in 1976 with the New York Cosmos, becoming arguably the first world-class player to leave a top-flight club side for the NASL while still in his prime. This probably explains his outstanding success in the USA. He was top scorer in the NASL on four occasions and would be the league's all-time leading scorer. In 1981, the Italian Welshman would win the NASL 'Most Valuable Player Award'.

Chinaglia was never enamoured with the American supporters while with the Cosmos. He was outspoken, and his flight from Italy to the NASL started a rift within the Italian-American population of New York. Many were, of course, pleased and excited to have Chinaglia play in their hometown; others saw him as a traitor to Italy, feeling he had a duty to remain in his native land to help Italy win the World Cup in 1978. The split became painfully overt during a home game in the Giants Stadium, when a Cosmos supporter paid for an aircraft to overfly the stadium during the game, tugging a banner that proclaimed: 'Giorgio Stinks!'

This said, gorgeous Giorgio scored 193 goals in his 213 NASL appearances and, in 2000, he was inducted into the USA National Soccer Hall of Fame. I saw him play several times in America and his class stood out. Incredible fitness coupled with a high level of skill and exceptional vision was nearly always too much for his opponents. A hatful of fine-quality goals enhanced the American game almost immeasurably.

He worked with ABC during their coverage of the 2006 World Cup and he currently hosts a weekly soccer talk show, *The Football Show*, on Sirius Satellite Radio. On the down side, on Friday, 13 October 2006, an arrest warrant was issued for Chinaglia after investigations about extortion connected to shares in Lazio.

NENE

Teófilo Juan Cubillas Arizaga is considered the greatest Peruvian footballer ever. He was born on 8 March 1949 near Puente Piedra, Lima. Nicknamed 'Nene' (baby), Teófilo started his pro soccer life at the age of 16 with the Peruvian club Alianza Lima. Four years later, he was part of the Peru national team that got to the last eight of the 1970 World Cup in Mexico, scoring five of his nation's nine goals in the process. He came out of the tournament being considered an equal to Jairzinho, Müller, Beckenbauer and Rivera and was compared with a young Pelé. In 1972, Nene was elected as the South American Footballer of the Year.

In 1973, Teófilo joined FC Basel for a fee of around £15,000. But life in Switzerland was not for him, the game there being a highly systemised affair that didn't so much as neglect his flair but made little room for him to express himself. He moved to FC Porto, muttering that the Swiss played like cuckoo clocks. The Portuguese club paid approximately £300,000 for his services, the club chairman boasting that he had bought 'gold for silver'.

Peru failed to qualify for the 1974 World Cup in West Germany but, in 1975, Nene helped his country to runners-up spot in the South American Championship. In the semi-finals, he scored two goals in Peru's 3–1 defeat of Brazil.

In Argentina during the 1978 World Cup, Peru fought their way into the second round. Nene scored five of Peru's seven goals in the tournament. He hit two outstanding goals in the opening match against Scotland, the first from a free-kick. Peru were held by the powerful Dutch side but Nene scored a hat-trick in the next game against Iran, including two penalties.

His ten goals in World Cup Finals make him the highest-scoring Peruvian ever in that competition. He netted 26 times in 81 games for Peru, and no one has ever bettered that record.

Nene then rejoined his first club Alianza, but in 1979 moved to the Fort Lauderdale Strikers and, over five NASL seasons, he scored 65 times, including, in 1981, a seven-minute hat-trick against the Los Angeles Aztecs.

Although called up to help Peru in the 1982 World Cup in Spain as his country's first-choice striker, he hung up his boots that year, but he came out of retirement to play for Alianza Lima, after the whole team were killed in a plane crash on 8 December 1987, the worst disaster in the history of Peruvian football in terms of player loss of life. Nene played a few games, primarily as a mark of respect for the men who were lost in the crash, but also looking to give the club's supporters hope for the future.

Nene now lives in Coral Springs, Florida, where he owns a youth football camp. He was the only Peruvian named by Pelé as one of the 125 greatest living footballers in March 2004.

PHIL WOOSNAM – THE WELSH WIZARD

Phil Woosnam was born in Caersws, Montgomeryshire, in scenic mid-Wales, on 22 December 1932. For many, he was thought of in his playing days as a footballing genius who, from inside-right, almost without help, guided the fate of West Ham United during the crucial seasons of the late 1950s and early 1960s, between the Hammers' successful promotion campaign and consolidation of their position in the top flight of English football.

Phil was the first Hammer to play for Wales since Wilf James in 1932. A comparative latecomer to the game, he did play one match for Manchester City in 1952, having joined the Maine Road men for trials but holding on to his amateur status. Woosnam's skill was obvious from his earliest years. He advanced from Montgomeryshire Schoolboys to turn out at schoolboy, youth and full international level for Wales.

Phil won a scholarship to the University of Wales at Bangor and it was during his college career, in 1951, that he was awarded the first of eight amateur caps, playing his debut game at Bangor against England. He also skippered the Bangor varsity side to the Welsh Universities' Championship and graduated with a BSc Honours degree in Physics, Maths and Education.

Beyond the campus, Woosie (as he was known to his fellow players at Upton Park and the West Ham fans of the early 1960s) played for Wrexham, Peritus, Manchester City, amateur Sutton United and Middlesex Wanderers, before joining the Royal Artillery, where he rose to the rank of Second Lieutenant. While in the military, he was selected to play for the Army XI alongside Maurice Setters (of West Bromwich Albion) and Eddie Colman and Duncan Edwards (Manchester United).

It was with Leyton Orient that Woosnam's football career really got off the ground, but while at Brisbane Road Phil taught physics at Leyton County High School. He represented the London XI against Lausanne Sports while a player for the 'Os' and was named Amateur Footballer of the Year for 1955.

In November 1958, West Ham paid £30,000, a record fee at the time, to convince their near neighbours to allow their ace performer to move to Upton Park; he gave up teaching and made his debut at the Boleyn Ground against Arsenal in the same month. He had signed as a professional with Orient, but it wasn't until he had come to West Ham as a 26-year-old that he felt free to focus full-time on football.

Not many professional players have fitted so much into their lives as Phil has, certainly not by such a young age, although he was comparatively mature to be starting in first-class soccer. Phil was selected for Wales as an Orient player (in 1958 against Scotland) and while still an amateur. He went on to play for the Welsh full international team 14 times in his four years with West Ham, and he made 38 appearances at all the five then existing levels of the national teams of Wales, and had represented the Football League against the Italian League in Milan in 1960.

When Ron Greenwood took over from Ted Fenton as West Ham manager in 1961 (Phil had stood in as temporary manager between the departure of Fenton and the arrival of Greenwood), he brought with him an ethos of encouraging players to take coaching qualifications and Phil earned his English Football Association coaching licence in the early 1960s and then served on the Association's coaching staff for five years from 1962 to 1966. Like dozens of other former Hammers, Phil was influenced by the approach and philosophy of the England manager-to-be. According to the former West Ham manager, 'Phil was a very intelligent player. He was tactically aware and, having played at all sorts of levels as an international, was very much what I call a "cultivated" player. He was always going to do well in coaching because he was a natural teacher and enjoyed that side of things and I think he learned a lot at West Ham.'

This latter conclusion was backed up by John Lyall, who said, 'Woosnam used West Ham like a university and he had a good tutor in Ron. Of course, he took all that to America with him and you can see how the influence spread, particularly around the better clubs there. West Ham had always gone down well with American crowds when the club had tours there; it was the way we played, move it about, open, attack-oriented. That, of course, was a sort of signature of the game in America.'

In March 1962, Greenwood brought Johnny Byrne to the East End for another record fee, and this may have hastened Woosnam's departure from Upton Park. There were more than a few who saw Phil's transfer to Aston Villa as a real loss, as he and Byrne appeared to be building a dangerous understanding in the Irons attack. Phil had played 163 games for the Hammers and scored 29 goals. He won two more caps while at Villa Park and scored 23 goals in 111 League matches for the Villains.

In 1966, Woosnam emigrated to the United States to join the Atlanta Chiefs as general manager and player-coach. Two years on, in only their second year as a club, the Chiefs won the North American Soccer League under his leadership, the first ever national professional sports championship for Atlanta.

That same year, Phil was named NASL Coach of the Year and was appointed as coach of the US World Cup 1970 team which qualified against Canada and Bermuda in 1968 to play in the second round in 1969.

Phil resigned from both coaching positions and took on the job of reconstructing a nationwide professional league as

Executive Director and Commissioner of the NASL, a position he filled from 1969 to 1983.

During the 1969 season, Phil adopted the United Soccer Association's tactic of deploying overseas clubs while constructing domestic teams with a view for them to take over as soon as possible. As such, the 1969 NASL season looked and felt like both the USA and the IFA. British League sides were imported to represent the five NASL teams – Aston Villa took on the mantle of Atlanta; Kilmarnock metamorphosed into the St Louis Stars; West Ham once more were the Baltimore Bays; Dundee United the Dallas Tornado; and Wolverhampton Wanderers wore the livery of the Kansas City Spurs.

About halfway through the season, the 'real' American clubs had their identities returned to them and played their stand-ins in a short tournament. This was followed by the five home-grown teams contesting a 16-match programme, with Kansas City becoming the eventual winners of the league.

But, before that happened, the Baltimore Bays withdrew from the NASL. This left just four clubs and the prospect of putting together a programme looked ridiculous. Keeping quiet about Baltimore's demise, Phil talked the Washington Darts and the Rochester Lancers into withdrawing from the semi-pro American Soccer League (considered as the American Second Division) and the 1970 season started with half-a-dozen clubs on board. It didn't look massively impressive but, in the future, the 1970 season would be seen as a turning point for the NASL and American soccer in general. From an office in the basement of Atlanta Stadium, Phil took the NASL into the 1970 season.

In 1970, Rochester Lancers took the League Championship, with Kansas City going bust as the season concluded.

Before the start of the 1971 season, Phil persuaded Warner Brothers Communications to invest in the NASL, and the New York Cosmos came into the world. Two Canadian teams were also recruited – the Toronto Metros and Montreal Olympic. The three teams paid $25,000 each to play in the league and, for the first time, the North American Soccer League achieved a level of stability.

The eight-team NASL would form the foundation of the league that would draw adequate crowds and attract some of the game's greatest players to teams in cities throughout North America. No one would have recognised it at the time, but the fact of the matter was that a Hammer had saved American football, a game without a history in the 'New World' context, and given it a future. Clive Toye, in the role of second-in-command to Lamar Hunt and Woosnam, would remain with the NASL in some capacity for the rest of the league's existence.

The North American Soccer League would become by far the most successful professional soccer league in United States history, also expanding into Canada. It improved its status and performance in almost every way in successive seasons and, in 1975, Pelé, coming out of retirement, helped the league present a new and more dynamic profile. However, his signing by the New York Cosmos had a huge negative impact on the future of the league. More clubs signed international stars to keep up. The quality of play and attendance increased, but player salaries spiralled at an even faster pace. The rapid increase in attendance prompted the league to expand to 24 teams for 1978, and this marked the beginning of the end for the NASL.

By 1978, Phil had reinvented and expanded the league from 5 to 24 franchises, situated throughout Canada and the United States, and inaugurated the Trans-Atlantic Cup, an annual tournament involving the two best NASL teams and two leading clubs from overseas.

Apart from his work with the NASL, Phil was Vice-President of the United States Soccer Federation from 1969 to 1983. In the early 1970s, he came up with the idea of recruiting Pelé to the ranks of the New York Cosmos and, in 1975, the world's greatest footballer became the spokesperson and image for soccer in North America.

Phil managed the US Bicentennial Cup in 1976. This competition brought Brazilian, English and Italian national teams together with an All-Star United States side in a gala show of soccer that captured the international imagination, and it was hoped that the tournament would promote the game to the American audiences at a national level. Woosnam's NASL All-Star team were dubbed 'Team America', and became the focus of more than 500 media reporters who covered the event.

The men Phil brought together were pretty well representative of the NASL of the mid-1970s, being a mixture of ageing stars from overseas, some naturalised Americans – such as Julius (Julie) Vee, Steve David, John Kowalski, Alex Skotarek and Hank Liotart – and a small number of token US-born players – such as Arnie Mausser and Bob Rigby, both goalkeepers, Bobby Smith and Peter Chandler. Woosnam's squad hailed from a dozen countries and included Pelé, George Best, Bobby Moore, Rodney Marsh, Dave Clements and Giorgio Chinaglia. Good friends Best and Marsh stipulated that they started all three games but, when coach Ken Furphy refused, they both left the squad.

The first game of the tournament in Washington DC – Team America v Italy – attracted a crowd of 33,000 spectators. The 'home' side's performance reflected the fact that they came together without much preparation; looking something worse than disorganised, they were beaten 4–0. Team America played their second game in Seattle against Brazil and, although defeated 2–0, the 'mercenary' side looked a much improved outfit and were in the game for the full 90 minutes. On 31 May, the NASL lads met England in Philadelphia. Stewart Scullion scored Team America's only goal of the tournament as England won 3–1, but this was Team America's best performance of the three and provided a truthful reflection of the position of American soccer; tremendous potential but an awfully long way to go. However, overall the tournament was a huge success with big, enthusiastic crowds, averaging over 45,000, accompanied by generous press coverage both in the USA and throughout the world.

Released from his duties as Commissioner of the NASL in 1982, Phil became managing director of the marketing arm of US Soccer. In New Jersey in that year, Phil managed the FIFA World All-Star game at Giants Stadium, an event that was linked to the former Hammer's ambition for the USA to host the World Cup. Recruiting the likes of Henry Kissinger, Pelé and Franz Beckenbauer to this cause in 1983, Phil led the NASL to organise a bid for the 1986 World Cup. Although this fell short, as adviser to the USSF President, Phil played a crucial role in the successful 1987 bid for the USA to act as host for the 1994 World Cup.

When the 1994 World Cup Finals were staged in the USA, it was a testament to the foundations that Phil and others had laid in the country. Woosie must have been one of the most satisfied spectators at the tournament.

From 1983 to 1990, Woosnam chaired the company managing the USSF marketing. He became a consultant to Britain's ITV coverage of the 1994 World Cup and served on the Atlanta Committee for the Olympic Games (ACOG) as venue competition manager in Athens, Georgia. This was where the 1996 Olympic soccer semi-finals and finals for both men and women were staged at the 86,000-seat University of Georgia's 70-year-old Sanford Stadium, home of the Georgia Bulldogs grid-iron football team.

It is ironic that Phil almost didn't move to the USA. It was during the 1994 World Cup that he said, 'I wanted to continue my playing career in Division One and, one week after agreeing to join Atlanta Chiefs, Tommy Docherty asked me to join him at Chelsea. I hadn't signed anything with Atlanta, but I had given them my word and I stuck to it. But more than once I moaned, "Why didn't you come in for me earlier?" at Chelsea.' Everyone involved in American soccer might be thankful for Stamford Bridge's loss.

With in excess of 30 years of soccer leadership in the American context, Phil Woosnam has been one of the major contributors to the growth and development of soccer at all levels in the United States. He was inducted into the US National Soccer Hall of Fame on 14 June 1997, having previously been inducted into the Georgia Soccer Hall of Fame on 10 January 1997.

Phil is now a naturalised American citizen, and he and his wife Ruth, the administrator of the USSF and NASL Referee programmes from 1969 to 1978, now live in Dunwoody, Georgia, a northern suburb of Atlanta.

BOBBY HOWE

Bob Howe was born in Chadwell St Mary, Essex – very much West Ham country – on 22 December 1945. An outstanding talent at half-back for Thurrock and Essex and London Schoolboys, Bob signed as an apprentice at Upton Park and became a full professional with West Ham in December 1962. He was part of the Hammers' Youth Cup-winning side the following year.

Bob came on as substitute in a 2–2 draw at home against Southampton in September 1966 but didn't make his first start until another 18 months later in a goalless draw at home to Coventry City. He came into the first team at left-back after Frank Lampard broke his leg.

According to Bob, he always did well at Coventry. He had waited a long time to start a first-team game. In fact, he'd got to the stage where he was regularly knocking on the manager's door. But Ron Greenwood would ask the young man to take a seat, talk for a while and Bob would come out thinking he'd had a good conversation, but then was left wondering what it had all been about. In retrospect, Bob saw that this was a good way of defusing the situation.

But Bob had no thoughts of leaving West Ham; his main motivation was to get into the Hammers first team. For him, without that driving ambition, players lose something in their play; ego is needed to fire the belief that one's aims are credible.

Although Bob didn't get many goals as a player, when he did score it was all the more special for him. He played around 50 per cent of his first-team games as a defender, but he recalls the best goal he scored was a volley from the edge of the box against Peter Bonetti of Chelsea, at what was then the South Bank end (now the Bobby Moore Stand) of the Boleyn Ground, in August 1970. West Ham drew that match 2–2.

One game that sticks in Bob's memory was when West Ham were massacred 5–2 at Old Trafford. He recalled that the Hammers didn't play particularly badly, but United played very well. George Best scored a hat-trick and played unbelievably throughout the match. The West Ham players sat on their coach, waiting to leave the ground, when Bob saw Best running from a doorway, trying to reach his Ferrari while being chased by a pack of young girls.

The other game that Bob recalls most vividly was when he played against Pelé in Randalls Island, New York. It was an exhibition game against Santos. He recalled sensing the adrenalin rush, three or four hours before the game, just thinking about having to mark players like Best and Pelé. Bob played at the back and had to man-mark the great Brazilian. Howe had pulled a quadricep muscle in a game immediately prior to the meeting with Santos, but he had it strapped up because he could not have contemplated missing that match.

Bob played well, but Pelé scored two goals. For Howe, his experience of playing against great players tells him that they always have a choice whether they play well or not. He recognised he couldn't do anything against Pelé, but in that same game Clyde Best scored two goals and Bob's team drew 2–2. After the match, Pelé thanked Bob for not kicking him.

At wing-half, Bob served West Ham well for five years, making 82 appearances and scoring four times. He played with some of the greatest names of English football while at Upton Park, including Jimmy Greaves, Billy Bonds, Trevor Brooking and Bobby Moore, and Bob sees himself as being very lucky to have been a Hammer during a time when the Boleyn Ground was graced by such high standards of professional play, although he recognises that the side underachieved. He is also proud to have played against the likes of Bobby Charlton and George Best.

Early on, Bob felt a little overawed surrounded by such big-name players but, when he played alongside them, he generally found that they weren't only superb footballers but also great people, making him feel welcome and helping him wherever they could.

Bob recalls Bobby Moore being a model captain and the person everybody aspired to be, particularly defenders like Bob. However, as far as Bob was concerned, no one could emulate Moore, because he was such an immaculate player, and he cherished the experience of playing alongside him.

Bob was a great fan of John 'Budgie' Byrne and recalled

how he used to get some of the other younger players out on the forecourt of Upton Park. John organised the youngsters in five-a-side games, during one of which Budgie closed the big iron gates leading out to Green Street and got the lads to chip long balls to him. He would control each one on his chest and volley it, on the turn, at the gates; not one shot ended up on Green Street. Bob recalled how Byrne had tremendous ball skills and saw him as a model for younger players in terms of his talent. For Bob, Byrne's control and appreciation of where people were was unbelievable.

While he was enjoying rubbing shoulders with the first-team stars, the 16-year-old Bob was also studying for his O-levels. He thought it would be great to put away his books and just play football every day, but Bob remembers how the apprenticeship system at that time was a very important part of a youngster's football education.

Although Howe was something of a schoolboy football star, playing for his county and London, as an apprentice pro he had to start again. Bob remembers picking up the dirty kit worn by the first team and having to clean out their dressing room. At that time, the first-team players changed in one dressing room and the youth-team boys changed in another. The only time that a younger player could get into the first-team changing room was to gather up their sweaty gear and make sure it was washed. So the aim of budding players was to bridge the divide and get from one dressing room to the other – to hang their own clothes up. In retrospect, Bob sees this as useful psychology and a good principle for young players to learn, humility being its own lesson.

For Bob, when a player came to Upton Park as a youth and then an apprentice, the expectation was to aspire to play in the reserves; the apprenticeship process and the reasons for it were understood and, looking back, he sees the good grounding and attitude this inspired.

Bob gives Ron Greenwood a great deal of credit for his development, and recalls how he always encouraged his players to coach. According to Bob, that gave the West Ham players a greater appreciation of the game and provided them with valuable experience for later career development. For Bob, coaching in the schools as a young player also gave him the opportunity to earn some extra money; players' wages were not massive at that time. On signing as an apprentice, he was paid £5 per week and this was raised to £12 when he signed as a professional. Adding his coaching wages, he could almost double his income. However, Bob admits to having been in America for so long he is unable to remember what he would have been earning later in his playing years.

Bob played in every position for West Ham except goalkeeper, but was mainly a wing-half in the old 'W' formation. He was better on the left side, even though he was naturally right-footed. He played more as a left-sided midfield player as opposed to an outside-left, like, for instance, John Sissons. He would tend to drop back deeper in a more defensive midfield role, but probably his best position was left-back; he was quick over short distances and had sharp reflexes, enabling him to respond quickly in deed and thought.

Bob took his full coaching badge at Lilleshall in 1968. For Howe, it was a wonderful experience. Bobby Robson took him through their Preliminary course, although Gordon Jago was his instructor, while Dario Gradi did a great job as Bob's instructor when he gained the full badge. Bob was privileged to have rubbed shoulders with and learned from some of the best coaches and managers the English game was to produce in the second half of the 20th century.

Bob coached in the schools four days a week, Monday to Thursday. Greenwood discouraged his players from working on Fridays, given that they would probably have to play the following day.

The players did a good job in Newham, one of the poorest of the London boroughs and the home of West Ham Football Club. The head of one of the local schools, Ashburton, was so impressed that he once contacted Greenwood to ask if any of his players would be interested in going back there to run their PE department in the summer.

Bob has recalled that the players of his generation had more time off in the close season than current players. He would spend the summer teaching football, cricket and other games he just invented to enliven what he was doing with young players. He remembers this as a really good experience. Bob worked with fellow Hammer and brother-in-law-to-be Trevor Hartley (who is married to Bob's sister Julie) but, when the latter returned to Holloway School, Clyde Best joined Bob at Ashburton. It is hard to imagine a Premiership manager asking his first-team stars to give up their afternoons to coach local schoolchildren today; as Bobby says, it would be nice to think they would do it for free, as it is unlikely that any would need the extra money.

For Bob, it's dangerous for a young sportsman to have a lot of time and a lot of money on their hands (this was often proven at West Ham during the 2006/07 season) and he feels this is the route of the trouble some find themselves getting into.

Bob has memories of talking to John Lyall when the Irons' manager of the future went to watch him training at West Ham years ago. He remarked that he thought young players had got softer in their approach, and talked about one youngster who failed to turn up for training because his mum couldn't drive him there. When Bob first arrived at West Ham, he was obliged to undertake two walks of ten minutes each, two buses and a train to get there. And he had to make sure he was always early because he wanted a decent ball to practise with. In those days, the balls were often over-inflated or misshapen and the training gear was only washed once a week.

Of course, that's all changed for the better but, for Bob, that atmosphere and the apprenticeship system of old is sorely missed. He doesn't want to enslave young men, but perhaps enable them to feel a little more conscious of being a servant to their club and use this as part of their learning process.

Having played in the first team, Bob found the opportunities at Upton Park became less frequent and he came to the conclusion that it would be better to move on and he saw himself as being fortunate to go to AFC

Bournemouth where he would conclude his playing career in the English League. The transfer fee of £30,000 was quite a decent sum for Bournemouth at that time.

Although the Cherries were in the Third Division at the time, they were pushing hard to reach the old Second Division and Bob saw his move to Dean Court as a good one. Trevor Hartley was on the coaching staff there and Bob saw the man who took him to the south coast, John Bond, as a good young manager. Bob recalled how the ex-West Ham defender wore his heart on his sleeve, so players always knew his mood and he was not slow to make his intentions and opinions clear.

Bond loved giving team-talks; it was a stage for him, and he was a gifted orator in that context (even now at former-player gatherings it is Bond who most often speaks for his fellow veterans). Bond was another manager who had learned from his long acquaintance with Ron Greenwood, and would painstakingly outline the role that he wanted each of his players to follow based on the reports he had of the opposition.

Bond also had a collection of motivational clichés. He'd usually hold a team meeting around noon if they were playing away. One day, the squad were at a hotel that had a lecture hall, which the players saw as an invitation for Bond to make even more of a meal of his team-talk opportunities. The players got to the hall a little bit before their manager and one of their number wrote a list of around ten of John's usual sayings and catchphrases on the blackboard behind the stage from where Bond would be delivering his sermon; the player pulled down a screen in front of the list so that John wouldn't know what was written behind it.

Individual odds were also listed against the particular expression, and the players were making bets between themselves on what their manager's first cliché of the day would be – the 'wife and kids' one, where John would remind his players that they were doing this not only for themselves, but also for their families. Or would it be the 'nice car' one, where he would equate success on the field to the opportunity of becoming the proud owner of a Jaguar? Bond had all these different strategies to try to lift the team, but Bob was sure it lifted Bond, too. The list, in the end, remained veiled.

For Bob, Bond could make a man feel like the best player on earth after a win but, on losing, his disappointment was felt by everybody. There was no grey between the black and white for Bond; he was a man of extremes, but Bob got on well with him. Howe appreciated where John came from (a poor Essex family and football by the long route) and thought his manager appreciated what Bob had learned from his time at West Ham. Howe liked to chat to Bond away from the game, although the two men always talked about the game and, for Bob, the former Hammers defender was great company.

Bond played the 'West Ham way' at Bournemouth and Bob saw little difference from what he'd become accustomed to at Upton Park. It was frenetic, initially, fighting away in a tough division, but, once he got used to it, Bob was satisfied with the situation. Bond was always looking to improve the quality of the club both on and off the field and the likes of Howe could feel Greenwood's influence on their manager, although, of course, they were different personalities.

For Howe, Bond was a gifted manager who, alongside another Upton Park favourite, Ken Brown, pushed Bournemouth right up to the club's potential. Bob saw Brown as a brilliant assistant for Bond, although 'Topper' was never serious for long. For all this, the players understood that he was serious about his football, and knew how much he cared about what they and the club were doing. The Brown–Bond combination brought the senior players like Bob, John Benson, Mel Machin and Fred Davis into conversations about the team and the way they played and Howe never felt that his manager was paying the players lip service, as John would often act on what they said. For Bob, this teamwork attitude was an art, in that Bond could ask for advice yet continue to command the respect of the players.

At the time, Bournemouth had an exciting team that included Ted McDougall as the main striker. The Scot scored a lot of goals before he joined Manchester United, and McDougall would later play for West Ham. Bob enjoyed the style of football the Cherries played and the buzz around the place. After several games in midfield for Bournemouth, he eventually settled in the left-back spot.

At the age of 28, Bob was advised to retire. As he had his coaching qualifications, and knew Hartley (who was coaching at Dean Court) very well, that was his path into a coaching career.

Bob Howe had played professionally for 12 years in

England and coached the youth teams at Bournemouth and Plymouth Argyle, but, with his long-time friend Harry Redknapp, he decided to try to develop his career in the United States.

Bob and Harry had joined the club at the same time and they played a lot together in the youth ranks at West Ham. The two were in the side that won the FA Youth Cup in 1963 and they played together in the Southern Junior Floodlit Final. More than 17,000 fans turned up to watch the second leg of the Youth Cup Final against Liverpool that the Hammers won 6–5 on aggregate. It was a tremendous feat, West Ham having gone into the game 3–1 down; it was 2–2 at half-time in the return game, and the young Irons knew they had to score three goals in the second half to win the Cup.

Harry and Jimmy Gabriel had joined Bournemouth at around the same time at the end of the 1971/72 season. They lived literally across the street from each other in a new development at Christchurch; Bob lived just 100 yards away, so the three took it in turns to drive to training. It was nearly always nerve-racking when it was Harry's turn to drive but, according to Bob, that's the way Redknapp lived his life – on the edge.

Harry and Jimmy were very much into coaching. Jimmy went to the United States in 1974, and he took Harry there in 1975/76 to play for him at Seattle Sounders. Jimmy was only the assistant manager then, but, when the manager left to take over Vancouver Whitecaps, Jimmy became the head coach of Seattle and asked Harry and Bobby to become his assistants. Harry would spend the summers in Seattle and return to England in the winter to scout for the Sounders, while Bob remained in America all year round.

Redknapp was mainly responsible for the reserve team and younger players at Seattle, but he was always trying to stay one step ahead of the game, always looking at what the opposition did and studying the league tables to know what the team needed to do. Again, the influence of Ron Greenwood was tangible.

Some years ago, John Lyall and Bob were responsible for a group of West Ham players on their Preliminary coaching badge as instructors. Harry was part of that group. Bob recalled him being terrific, knowing the game well but also knowing players, and how they could work with each other on and off the field.

Bob recollected that Redknapp went with Jimmy Gabriel to Arizona in preparation for the ASL but the club never got off the ground, so Harry came back and went to work with Bobby Moore at Oxford City. Bob was amused by the contradiction – Harry at Oxford!

According to Bob, playing with Redknapp in the Hammers youth team of the early 1960s, he would never have imagined that he would go on to become one of the Premiership's longest-serving managers. But when he came to Seattle, he flowered as a coach, having plenty of opportunities to express himself.

Bob saw how Harry, like many other West Ham players, was able to take advantage of his early experience of coaching in the schools; that background of working with kids and developing coaching styles was something that both Bob Howe, Redknapp and a whole generation of Hammers benefited from and, in return, passed on to the young men of the East End who were amazed to see their idols playing with and coaching them.

In 1977, both men became players/assistant coaches with Seattle Sounders in the NASL (Redknapp had played for Seattle the previous year). Harry eventually returned to England for good, but Bob stayed on in America to become the director of coaching for the Washington State Youth Soccer Association, which prepared him for a position with US Soccer.

Bob became assistant coach to the US men's U-17 team and, by the early 1990s, he was managing the Under-18 side. Howe coached the US U-20 men's national team in the 1993 FIFA World Youth Championships, leading the side to a fine 6–0 victory over European Champions Turkey in the opening round.

Bob then became the director of coaching education for the United States Soccer Federation, a post he held for four years, but his expectations for the role proved to be more advanced than the people he was working for; the job became much too administrative for his liking. He was also working in Chicago while his wife, Sheree, was living in Seattle, where he'd lived for most of his time in the States.

Bob edited the USSF's official guide for coaches through six levels of certification, combining State and national levels. He was recommended by his former team-mate Clive Charles for the post of head coach with Portland Timbers, a club in the State of Oregon who were playing in the pro A-League.

He took up the post in 2001. It was ironic that he became the Timbers coach as they had maintained a strong rivalry with the Sounders in the days of the NASL.

Bob was A-League Coach of the Year in 2004 after winning the Championship with his team, who recorded 18 wins, seven draws and three losses that season. The Timbers also led the league in offence, scoring 58 goals, 14 more than the runners-up.

Bob recently reflected on the standard of soccer at this level, saying, 'It's difficult to compare standards, but I think we could give English Third Division teams a good run for their money. We average crowds of 6,000 and we are one level down from Major League Soccer, which is the top division in the US.'

Bob now lives in Lake Oswego, just seven miles outside Portland. He finds the lifestyle in America 'great' and he and his family are very happy. Bob has also kept in touch with former Hammers Harry Redknapp, Frank Lampard, Roger Cross and, up until he passed away, Clive Charles.

Bob Howe always looked to make the Timbers a model franchise in the A-League, to be competitive and also entertaining. But, like Clive Charles, he wanted the place where he worked to be a focal point and a resource for the education of coaches and players in the surrounding community. He has produced a coaching video and is a prolific author on the subject of coaching and youth soccer. He edited *Soccer: How to Play the Game: The Official Playing and Coaching Manual of the United States Soccer Federation*, by Dan Herbst (1999), and was the co-author, with Tony Waiters, of *Coaching 9-, 10- and 11-Year-Olds: The Golden Age of Learning* (1989) and *Coaching 6-, 7-, and 8-Year-Olds – The Coaching Series* (1988). Bob's feels his own work, *Coaching the Player* (1991), is a book he can build on, thinking that he has another coaching book in him. One of his most recent contributions to the literary world was as editor, in collaboration with Hank Steinbrecher and Dan Herbst, of *Soccer: How to Play the Game* (1999). These resources are widely used in coach certification and training programmes across the USA.

Although he has said that his life has been fairly one-dimensional, Bob sees himself as being fortunate because, to use his phrase, his 'vocation has also been his avocation'. Outside the game, Bob enjoys golf and is always looking to improve his handicap. He likes to return to Britain every two years to call on family and old friends.

To the amazement of many long-term fans, Portland let Bob go in mid-October 2005. The USL First Division franchise said it had relieved Bob of his coaching duties. It was said that a change was needed as Bob's style was not working when the Timbers went into the playoffs. Bob had coached the team to a division title the previous year and left the Timbers with a regular season record of 68 wins, 20 draws and 50 losses in five seasons. The team made the playoffs four times in those five seasons, but made it past the first round only once. Bob's playoffs record was three wins and seven losses. As such, his regular season record was not bad, but it was thought that better form was required to become Champions of this USL First Division.

Bob had helped turn the Timbers into a team with a devoted fan base. Members of the 'Timbers' Army' had turned Portland's match days into well-attended and colourful events. John Cunningham, the team's president, said that Bob Howe had been 'instrumental in helping shape the franchise during its first five seasons'.

When Bob departed, the Timbers said goodbye to the only coach and general manager the team has ever had. Bob became the coaching director for Emerald City FC in Washington State a month later, following the club's two-year nationwide search for the right person to fill the position. Emerald let it be known that they recognised the fact that Howe had dedicated his life to the game and that the club was fortunate to have his passion, experience and leadership to guide them on a path to excellence.

Bob's career in the United States has enabled him to coach and to educate at the highest levels of the game and he has been able to call upon that experience to instruct in educational programmes throughout the USA. But, for Bob Howe, the emphasis in the States on playing recreational soccer for fun has the most resonance because he admits that football has always been fun for him… and that the most fun he ever had was playing the game at West Ham.

5

CLYDE CYRIL BEST

'Clyde Best was a phenomenally good player – big, strong, fast, yet light on his feet and very skilful. I always thought he'd have made a great centre-half one day, but I don't think that was for Clyde because he loved to score goals… and, of course, he was very good at that, too. He was aggressive but was able to channel that. Off the field, he was a gentle giant, always ready to listen and learn. He also turned out to be a good coach. I think that's because people were ready to listen to him. He had a commanding presence.'

RON GREENWOOD – WEST HAM AND ENGLAND

'Clyde used to come to our school to train us – him and another player, George Andrew. Clyde had a really broad accent and not even the Jamaican lads could make out everything he was saying, but Andrew was from Scotland and not only could he not understand

us – and "us" were Indian, Bangladeshi, African, West Indian, Jewish, dyed-in-the-wool Cockneys and one Native American kid – but we didn't have a clue what he was on about. I can still remember over at Southern Road playing field, Plaistow... there was Clyde running along, purring away instructions at us, with his coffee-cream tones, and Andrew, screaming a tirade of Highland expletives, but the only comprehensible sentence that echoed across the pitch was "WILL YE NAY STOOP SHOOTIN'!?"'

BRIAN BELTON

'In America, Clyde played with the best – Jimmy Greenhoff, Tommy Smith, Rodney Marsh and so on. And, of course, he was in Holland at a great time. But, as a striker, he had it all and, maybe if he'd have stayed in England a bit longer... who knows? It was touch and go in as far as him playing in the Cup Final in '75, although in the end it was Bobby Gould who got in the team. Bobby had that little bit more aggression and experience then and gave us a few more options in that team. It wasn't a call about who was the best player; it was making a decision about playing against Fulham with the players we had. They had a lot of experience, including Alan Mullery and Bobby [Moore], who knew Clive well. They were in a lower division and you needed to know that they were going to play like a team from that division. But you just can't do better than manage your country and Clive did that. He was a fantastic

92

player and there was no faulting his commitment. Everyone loved him, you couldn't do anything else! Everything about him said "friendliness".

'But that was deceiving on the pitch. He never lost it, but there were times when he'd literally run through a wall of defenders like a speeding bulldozer and score a goal that seconds earlier you would have not given anyone a chance of doing. He was a great asset when West Ham won a corner. Most of the defence would be watching him, knowing, if the ball come anywhere near him, no one had a chance of stopping him connecting.'

JOHN LYALL – WEST HAM UNITED

'Clyde's a lovely man. When he first came over, we had a few laughs with him, but he's one of the family and has been for years. We love him to bits. But he scared the pants off of some when he was playing. He was so big! See him running straight at you and it was all you could do just to stop yourself getting out of the way. Like a bleedin' great express train! Great to watch, though. The crowd loved him. There was no one else like him; come to think of it, there never has been. The closest is the other John Charles, the Welsh feller. Would have been a right old battle if the two of them had ever played against each other. I'd put me money on Clyde, though. Massive he was; shocking!'

JOHN CHARLES – WEST HAM UNITED

In the summer of 2000, I was among the crowd of around 2,000 in the wind and rain that swept in viciously from the Atlantic over the uncovered national stadium in Hamilton, Bermuda. These were not the conditions the likes of Judith Charmers had led me to expect; it was the World Cup at its most basic and raw. Bermuda were playing British Virgin Islands (BVI) and the home side were 7-0 up as Bermuda's teenage striker Stephen Astwood rounded the BVI's keeper and prepared to walk the ball into the net. But the forward stopped inches from securing the goal. Taking a quick look behind him and seeing not a hint of a threat, he got down on his knees and poked his head at the ball as he might a snooker cue, sending the ball trundling along the ground and into the net. The spectators appreciated what might have been a candidate for the most impudent goal in World Cup history but, on the bench, the man responsible for the Bermudan team was shaking his head, saying, 'Wait 'til I get hold of him... Ridiculous!' He complained that, if he had been a BVI defender, he'd have wanted to kick Astwood into the Atlantic after such a show of contempt.

The 9-0 result was to be Bermuda's biggest-ever victory in the World Cup; it completed a 14-1 aggregate scoreline. Two weeks earlier, Clyde Best was being threatened with dismissal for no apparent reason, or, at least, nothing that anyone could adequately articulate. Clyde was able to see the funny side of the situation and speculate that history might remember him as the first international coach to get the sack for winning matches.

Clyde Best would never have added insult to humiliation to

opponents in the way Astwood had. But Bermuda's most famous son had acquired a keen sense of the ludicrous in his role as the island nation's technical director of football.

In the days when international footballers from abroad were a rarity in the English game, and no black player had been capped for England, Clyde Best was a hero at Upton Park, filling in the gaps between Martin Peters, Geoff Hurst and Harry Redknapp. Clyde joined West Ham at a point in time when it looked to many as if the Hammers would take over from Tottenham as London's most fashionable club. In the late 1960s, fresh from FA Cup and European success, with three players at the hub of the World Cup-winning team, Best must have thought the world was literally at his feet when he arrived at the Boleyn Ground. He was rated by Ron Greenwood, the West Ham manager, as 'the best 17-year-old I've ever seen'.

Clyde has been called the 'Emile Heskey' of his day. But, while there is a similarity in the look of the two players, Best had a much more impressive goalscoring record than Heskey and a far greater physical presence. He certainly was exceptional. Before his days at the Boleyn Ground, Clyde had represented his country and won a silver medal at the 1967 Pan-Am Games. He had turned out for Bermuda in an Olympic qualifying tournament in 1966/67 and the first ever World Cup preliminary tournament in 1968; he would also take part in the qualifying stages of the 1970 World Cup.

Clyde was a powerful striker and he dwarfed everyone in the West Ham dressing room. But, despite his gargantuan proportions, he was astonishingly fast. In fact, he was an extremely graceful and beautifully balanced player. He scored a goal at Goodison Park having run from the halfway line with most of the Everton team hanging on to him. He had a potent shot and was a marvellous header of the ball.

At the time, Clyde Best was the only black player appearing regularly in first-team football in the English First Division. Brian Woolnough's book on black footballers – *Black Magic: England's Black Footballers* (1983) – is ostensibly a celebration of black players in the British game but, of Best, Woolnough commented, 'He is perhaps the best example of why it has taken so long for managers, coaches and the public to accept the coloured [*sic*] stars. Best would be brilliant one game, bad the next, and the question marks against the black players' stamina, power and determination hung over them for years.'

This does not really describe Clyde's performances for West Ham (and I saw most of the games he played for the Hammers) and, having interviewed close to a hundred former West Ham players, many of whom played and trained alongside Clyde, I have never heard him talked about in this way. No player worked harder than Clyde Best; his stamina was never a problem and, when compared to contemporaries, the likes of Ted McDougall, for instance, he looked like an endurance athlete.

In the final analysis, his record speaks for itself. In effect, Woolnough cobbles together a myth about Clyde at the same time as helping perpetuate another about black players in general.

Clyde Best was only the second black player to break into

the West Ham first team. On 2 April 1970, the East End Irons hosted a Division One game against Leeds United. That day, Clyde took the field with his great friend the defender John Charles. It was the full-back's final game for the club. This was the first time that the Hammers had included two black players in their line-up, and broke ground in terms of race and top-flight football in general. Best marked the occasion with a goal in the 2–2 draw.

In the 1971/72 season, Clyde scored 23 times in 56 outings; in 218 appearances for West Ham, Clyde scored 58 times, and his presence alone opened the doors for the likes of Hurst, Brooking and Bryan 'Pop' Robson; it often took two or three defenders to control Best, who was busily clearing the path for his striking colleagues. He remains Bermuda's most famous footballer and was the highest-profile black player in the late 1960s/early 1970s. He went on to play for the Tampa Bay Rowdies in the USA and rubbed shoulders with Pelé, Beckenbauer and George Best in the summer of 1975. That year, Clyde was voted 'Most Valuable Player' in the North American Soccer League, the season the Rowdies won the Championship. He once scored a hat-trick for the Rowdies – Pelé replied but only got two.

Best came back at Upton Park for a few games in 1975/76 but, looking for a new challenge, he joined Feyenoord in the Dutch First Division for two seasons. At that point, 'the people's club' were one of the top clubs in Europe. In 1974/75, they reached the Final of the UEFA Cup after a 4–3 aggregate victory over VfB Stüttgart in the semi-finals and met Tottenham Hotspur in the two-legged final. In the first leg at White Hart Lane, Spurs took a 2–1 lead, but Theo de Jong equalised with five minutes of the game remaining. Feyenoord won their home leg of the tie in Rotterdam 2–0 with goals from Wim Rijsbergen and Peter Ressel, to become the first Dutch team to win the UEFA Cup. However, for the remainder of the 1970s, Feyenoord won only one more honour, the Dutch Championship in 1974. After his spell in Rotterdam, Clyde returned to the NASL with Toronto Blizzard and Portland Timbers.

In 1997, Clyde took over control of the Bermudan national side as technical director. He and his wife Alfreida had given up their dry-cleaning business in California so that Clyde could return home as Bermuda's football saviour – or, as he put it, 'to put something back into the country which shaped me'. However, when he got back to his homeland, he found that the game was on its knees, still reeling from the scandal two years earlier when seven national team members were caught trying to smuggle drugs back into the country in the bottom of their shoes after a Pan-American Games qualifier. Sponsors had turned their backs on the game in droves and the national team had been effectively disbanded. Bermudan football needed a hero and there was only one real candidate; the prison warden's boy from rural Somerset in Bermuda, who had made them so proud when he left for England with little more than apprehension and a one-way ticket to Heathrow. Now the pioneer returned, having succeeded as a professional footballer in England, Holland, Canada and the USA.

To get some idea of the culture shock Clyde might have

experienced when he reached London's East End, you need to spend some time in Somerset, Bermuda, which was named after the English county of Somerset. I did just that.

Not actually part of the Caribbean, being 900 miles north of that area, Bermuda is 'British North America', according to the International Air Transport Association (IATA) and official British records. Although, in July 2003, Bermuda formally joined the Caribbean Community, as an Associate Member (non-voting); in certain areas, but not in others, it is a nominal British territory – nominal because, despite being British, it is self-governing internally, making all its own laws.

Until the mid-17th century, Bermuda was referred to as the 'Isles of Devils', as the reefs lying just below the surface of the waters surrounding it wrecked many a ship and their remains can still be found on the ocean floor.

Bermuda is a place of contradictions socially. By international standards, it has the highest marriage rates, but one of the lowest divorce rates. It has the biggest number of telephone lines, computers online and televisions per head. Bermuda's Gross Domestic Product is among the highest in the world, but its cost of living matches this status. It has (by a long way) the least generous benefits and services to its senior citizens and the disabled of any of the countries with a high GDP, but there's no illiteracy and essentially no pollution, no billboards, few racial problems, no graffiti, no litter, no rental cars, hardly any unemployment, drugs are not tolerated, and there are no nude or topless beaches.

At the start of the 21st century, Bermuda's average household income was $68,500 and, compared to regional neighbours like Puerto Rico, Jamaica and Haiti, no one in Bermuda is poor. But house prices in Bermuda are at least 300 per cent more expensive than comparative housing in the United States or Canada.

One of the oldest, smallest but most populated of the British Overseas Territories, and the oldest British Commonwealth member, Bermuda is also the fifth-smallest country in the world after Vatican City, Monaco, Nauru and Tuvalu. Bermuda has a land area of only 21 square miles (56 square kilometres). You can travel from one end of the country to the other in just over an hour and from north to south in 10–15 minutes. Going from north-west to east, the six principal islands are Ireland Island (north and south), Boaz Island, Somerset, Main, St David's and St George's; a 22-mile road will take you through all six. Much the largest island is Great Bermuda or Main Island (neither name is used locally; it is just referred to as 'Bermuda'). It is a mile wide on average, 14 miles long, and 259 feet above sea level at its highest point, with hills and fertile depressions.

Bermuda had no resident permanent population at all until 1609 when English settlers arrived by accident, with others joining them intentionally from 1612. Only a few stranded mariners had lived there previously. Bermuda had no natural resources, no gold or silver or anything else that could be mined or refined and, as a consequence, there was no basis for permanent population. However, the islands became the first place of disembarkation for slaves, labourers and those under sentence of penal transportation for assignment to America, and some inhabitants can trace their lineage back to those times. Today, Bermuda is both a tourist resort and offshore business centre; most people work in hotels, restaurants and stores.

Clyde Best was born in the island of Somerset. The small, picturesque, sleepy but friendly hamlet of Somerset Village is located on the far north-western tip of Bermuda, looking over a coast caressed by the waves of the North Atlantic. Somerset is one of the most enchanting villages in Bermuda. Only one main road goes through the village that is lined with typically quaint Bermudian pastel cottages, charming shops and inns on streets with names such as 'Spice Lily Lane' and 'Pink House Lane'.

Somerset Village is the centre of Sandys (pronounced 'Sands') Parish (Bermuda is divided into nine parishes and two municipalities) that is often referred to as Somerset. Sandys Parish has a population of 6,300 and encompasses the islands of Ireland, Boaz, and Somerset. Somerset Village is a mixture of quiet countryside, hillside views, craggy coastlines, sheltered coves, beaches, nature reserves, fishermen's coves, old fortifications, quiet winding lanes and peaceful villages.

Some visitors to Bermuda head straight for Sandys Parish and spend the whole of their stay there, feeling there is something unique about its rolling hills, lush countryside, and tranquil bays. Its isolation is part of its charm as is its tranquillity and unspoiled environment. It has traditionally kept a level of separation from the rest of Bermuda – for example, during the American Civil War most Bermudians sympathised with the Confederate States but Sandys Parish supported the Union.

All this is a long way from how Newham looked and felt in the late 1960s to Clyde Best, but there were similarities between East London and Bermuda that may have made the young player feel more at home – the East End and Bermuda are multicultural; 63 per cent of the population of Best's homeland are black, 33 per cent white and 4 per cent of Asian or other origin. Also, Bermuda is the third most densely populated state on Earth (behind Monaco and Singapore). So Green Street, on which the Boleyn Ground stands, crowded with shoppers and football fans on Saturday afternoons, would not have been too unsettling for the lad from Sandys.

Within months of his homecoming, Best had organised Bermuda's first International on home soil in five years. Links with the Premiership and Clyde's contacts in the United States, including the likes of Pelé and Harry Redknapp, brought back the funding and Clyde assembled a talented coaching team, all with precious little financial back-up from the game's administration in Bermuda. He was to recall how the Bermuda FA used to ask him to travel to training sessions using public transport. But he built a side out of bankers, teachers and construction workers good enough to beat Denmark's (the 1992 European Champions) Under-23 team.

For all this, it quickly became clear to Best that the task he had taken on was a massive one, but there would be little concrete appreciation of the massive efforts he would make. He lamented how the situation made him better understand the Biblical warning that prophets are without honour in their own land.

I met with Clyde during his occasional visits to East

London, bringing young players from the Bermuda Under-15s to work with the West Ham School of Excellence.

'I was born in Somerset, Bermuda, on 24 February 1951. I went to Churchill School in Hamilton, a boy's school. Earl (Gabby) Hart, he developed our soccer programme, but we come from playing in the streets. I played for Somerset. Graham Adams (an Englishman who knew Ron Greenwood) who was in charge of the national team at the time, selected me to play for Bermuda when I was 15. The old West Ham skipper, Phil Woosnam, was in America then. He probably saw me play and recommended me to West Ham and Ron Greenwood invited me to come over for a trial. Clubs in North America wanted me, but I didn't want to go there. West Ham was a good place to come to learn the art of soccer. We played the game the right way there... I don't know about now! But, after West Ham, I had spells with Tampa Bay Rowdies, Portland Timbers and coached college soccer in California.

'I returned to Bermuda to take up the job of coach/director of coaching. I was asked to come home to solve problems, which, over the years, had included lack of ambition, too few matches. Top players, like Manchester City's Shaun Goater and Kyle Lightbourne (who is now the Bermuda national coach) of Stoke, had been unavailable to play for their country. Around 2000, Bermuda were rated 163rd in the world – they are 161st now, just below Namibia and in front of Sierra Leone, but as a coach I was always optimistic about preparing the *country for the World Cup. We would like to be on a par with countries like the USA, Jamaica and Trinidad; we know we can do it. But our entire population is just over 65,000, that's fewer than a full house at Old Trafford, so it's going to be difficult, but size is of less importance than having players with ability in a well-organised team. There's talent, but it's got to be harnessed.*

'But I learned my trade in the right place. I think I bring a little bit of the East End to Bermuda. I saw Joe Cole a few years ago – he was a marvellous prospect, but we have youngsters with just as much ability as him. Shaun Goater, he did well at Manchester City, but there are a lot of others like him at home. There was midfielder Paul Cann, who came into the English game, and there were players turning out for top sides in the USA, like David Bascome at Harrisburg Heat. West Ham have always been very supportive. They know the kids.

'In my time as an international I didn't even count the times I played for Bermuda; I played a lot. They didn't keep records then. That's what happens when you're an amateur. At that time, we were similar to Denmark and Norway... we didn't have a professional set-up. If it had been professional, I would have been over the moon to have played, if it was like it is now... Things hardly changed for Bermuda up to the late '90s. We didn't enter the 1998 World Cup. We need to get the experience. It would be great to play England. Let the manager know that Bermuda is a lovely place to visit!

'In Bermuda, when I was a kid you didn't see much

television, but I used to watch grainy images of Spurs on the TV back home and that was the start of my ambition to play in England. I saw Spurs play and I said to myself, "Hey, what a beautiful way to earn a living..." and I was right. That's what got me interested in being a pro. At around the age of 12, I used to wait for the British ships to dock so I could play against the sailors in the matches they played.

'I arrived at Heathrow on a Sunday and there was nobody there to meet me. The club weren't expecting me until the Monday. Right then, I wished I'd never come. I thought I'd made the biggest mistake of my life. I managed to get the Tube to West Ham, not realising I needed Upton Park. It was getting late in the afternoon but a Hammers fan took this lonely, confused kid and directed me to a house owned by a lady called Michelle in Plaistow. She provided lodgings for a few of the young players at West Ham and I stayed with her for a while, and also at the Hartley Hotel, but after that I stayed at the family home of Clive and John Charles. When I arrived in England, now nearly 40 years ago, their mum was like a second mother to me. The Charleses are my extended family. John took me under his wing; he and Clive were like my brothers.

'Everybody at West Ham – from the chairman right down to Mrs Moss the tea lady – were unbelievable people. They taught us the importance of acting like a family; everyone pulled together. After games, we players would go to lunch, talk football, have a drink. There was a feeling of being a team and you took that out on the pitch. The atmosphere

and organisation was brilliant. Some of the people I was lucky enough to get to know have passed away now, but I believe they are up there looking down and are pleased to see the traditions they first started are maintained.

'I made my debut for West Ham in 1969, taking the number 7 shirt that had been the property of Harry Redknapp for much of the previous year. Arsenal were the guests at Upton Park that day. The match ended in a 1-1 draw. Roger Cross scored for us. I played 218 times between 1969 and 1975. It's hard to believe I played so many games for West Ham. Looking back, my time there seems so short.

'We had been beaten on the Saturday before my first game. Ron Greenwood came in on the Monday morning and he told me I was playing that evening. It was what you always wanted to do and you go and do it, just the best way you know how. But, with the team we had, it was easy to fit in. As young players, we had been brought up to play the right way, so adjusting wasn't a problem. Ron Greenwood was like a father to me. He helped me through the initial feelings of homesickness in my first few weeks in London and took a special interest in me. He had a feel for attacking football and worked with you on making your game better. All the time I was at West Ham, he continued working with me.

'I scored 58 goals for West Ham. The first was one of two in a game against Burnley in October 1969. West Ham won 3-1 at Upton Park. As a striker, you've got to be able to put the ball in the back of the net or you don't play. That was my fifth game for West Ham.

'It was just great to be at a club like West Ham. We had three World Cup winners and just to be there with them was unbelievable. My first day at the training ground, Ron organised it so I had a picture taken with the three of them. That was so exciting for me. In Bermuda, there are many fans of English football; most of them support Manchester United. But I let them know that West Ham were and still are the "Academy" of English football; look at the number of young West Ham players that have achieved greatness. They have come through the West Ham Academy. Ted Fenton laid the ground for this and Ron Greenwood and John Lyall built on it and Harry Redknapp kept it going. I played with Tony Carr in the youth team; he has done outstanding work nurturing the talent of young men to become good and great players.

'Looking back, it didn't really scare me coming to London; you are quite brash and confident when you are young. But I was very young to come and live in the East End of London. At such an age, that was quite incredible. In retrospect, it is hard to believe I managed to fit in and play alongside Bobby Moore and Geoff Hurst and everyone else – these were my heroes as a youngster. I watched the World Cup in 1966 and two years after that I was playing alongside these guys! That was like living your dream. Unbelievable really.

'I had my own version of the "Shaft" afro [in terms of style, Clyde was something of a Richard Rowntree look-alike in the early 1970s]. My dad was in charge of the prison at home. My mum was a housewife. I have five sisters and a *brother. One brother passed away. My second brother, Carlton, played football a bit, but we all played together when we were young. My daughter, Kimberley, she studied law in Buckingham and is now working for the Bank of Bermuda in investments. I've been married to Alfreida, who is also from Bermuda, for over 30 years.*

'East London was a different world to me. Bermuda has a population of less than 66,000. I played in front of nearly as many people at Old Trafford! Newham, where West Ham is, has about 250,000 people from all over the world.

' John [Charles] let me know about the kind of problems I might get from supporters away from Upton Park and how not to let it affect my game. You've got to remember, when I left home I was 17. I came to a strange country. Dealing with different people, different food, it was going to be different. When I look at it now, I think, Christ, how did I do that? I don't know!

'The first time I saw snow was at Portman Road. For a while, before the kick-off, I strolled around smiling and fascinated, catching the snowflakes. But, when you played against the likes of Leeds, you had to be strong. They'd kick yer! You had to be strong. It did help to be big and powerful, otherwise you just wouldn't have got through. If you're going to be a good soccer player, it's better to be big, rather than little. I was glad I was the size I was. It prevented me from getting injured.

'In Europe, you teach boys how to run and swivel on the ball, to try a trick or two. That rhythm comes naturally to our kids in Bermuda, but you need to put it together into

the structure of a team. We just have to start to invest some money and give the kids the exposure. Bringing them to England and letting them see first-hand what it takes is going to be a start.

'In Bermuda, people work hard for their money, but the wages are high. One of our biggest problems is that the people are just too nice for football. In the past, they have failed to work up sufficient aggression on the field – that's a major disadvantage. Part of my job was to try to alter that. When I was playing, I was, for some people, a bit too nice. During a West Ham tour in the States, I became quite popular. The tour finished up in Bermuda. I was treated like royalty when I came home and took the whole team to visit my family, at my home; it's near a quiet, sandy cove looking over the sea.

'In my first season I turned out 26 times for West Ham, scoring a handful of goals. West Ham finished 17th in the table, conceding 60 goals in the process, and in the third round of the FA Cup they were beaten by Middlesbrough, who were way down in Division Two at that time.

'The following season, in the first 13 games I had nothing to show in terms of goals. Things did get better towards the end of 1970; I scored five times in four matches, but, early in the New Year, West Ham were knocked out of the FA Cup, again in the third round, by Blackpool. The team that were relegated at the end of the season put four goals past us!

'Following the game, the press was full of the news that Bobby Moore, Jimmy Greaves, Brian Dear, myself and the

club physio Rob Jenkins had spent the evening before the match at Brian London's Blackpool nightclub; he had been heavyweight boxing champion of Britain. The thing was blown out of all proportion by West Ham and then the press. I never touched a strong drink while I was playing; all I'd had was orange. The others only had a few beers and we were in bed by 1.00am. But Ron Greenwood wanted to sack all of us! He was only prevented from doing so when he was over-ruled by the board.

'But the social life could have been our downfall sometimes. It was good. We were a friendly club; we worked hard and we played hard. We socialised, but, when the time came to play on the field, we played and meant it. I was friendly with everybody. It was a very family-type club. We were a part of a fraternity, so you're grateful.

'You have to thank Ron Greenwood for making West Ham into a family club. I think he did that very well. Greenwood stressed that we should look after each other. He instilled a lot of good habits in us; on the field and off. Even when Ron went upstairs and John Lyall took over, he still had a large say in the way the team played, the style we wanted to play. John was a chip off the old block anyway.

'It was roughly the same thing when he took over as manager. He, along with the likes of Ernie Gregory, also has to take a share of the credit for the way we all turned out. There was also Jack Turner, of course; he was my agent. Jack worked with many of the players, including Bobby Moore. He used to have his office near where I lived in Plaistow. Players, backroom staff, management – we all got on.

Clive Charles.

The supremely gifted Clyde Best (*top*) and Ade Coker (*bottom*) complete the trio of 'Onyx Odins'.

Top left: West Ham's Welsh Wizard and US soccer supremo to be Phil Woosnam – an Iron pumping iron at Upton Park. (England international and Norwich manager to be Ken 'Topper' Brown dozing off in the background.)

Top right: West Ham hero Harry Redknapp, who has enjoyed great success as a coach.

Bottom left: Hammer Bobby Howe – one of the creators of modern soccer in the USA.

Bottom right: Eusébio da Silva Ferreira… the 'Black Pearl'.

Top: Minnesota Kinks – Western Division Champions 1976. Ade Coker (*back row, third from left*). Former Busby Babe, coach Freddie Goodwin (*back row, second from right*) helped Manchester United win the 1956 and 1957 league championships. Geoff Barnet (*middle row, left end*) was best known in England as an Arsenal 'keeper. He became the coach of Kicks in 1981 but now runs a pub in his native Cheshire.

Bottom: December 2002 in Austin, Texas – the University of Portland women's soccer team hold the NCAA championship trophy aloft after a thrilling overtime victory.

Top left: Pilot Christine Sinclair, celebrating the winning goal, set NCAA records with 10 goals and 21 points in six games.

Top right: Olympic Gold medalist Brandi Denise Chastain. Although a member of Portland's deadly rivals during her college days, Brandi became a star of the American Women's soccer team working with Clive Charles from 1993 to '96.

Bottom: USA and former Tottenham Hotspur goalkeeper Kasey Keller.

West Ham's three claret, blue and black pioneers in action: Clive Charles (*top*); Ade Coker (*right*); and (*opposite page*) Clyde Best.

Bottom: The stage on which history was made – West Ham's Boleyn Ground (Upton Park).

Top: (*left to right*) Cobi Jones, head coach Steve Sampson, Clive Charles and Jeff Agoos enjoy a visit to the Eiffel Tower during the USA's France '98 World Cup campaign.

Bottom: Clive and his brother John, West Ham's first black player.

'I first wore a West Ham shirt playing as a youth in the Metropolitan League. I was big for my age and had started shaving when I was in my early teens. I think some people thought I was older but, to me, other kids looked too young, thin and scrawny. I played wide and on the right, keeping Harry [Redknapp] *out of the side for a while.*

'A great memory was when we played Santos in New York, latish in 1970... it was a friendly game. I got both of our goals and it ended 2-2. Pelé got the goals for Santos. Carlos Alberto skippered their team; Edu was a substitute. That was quite something at 19 for me.

'In the 1971/72 season, I scored 17 goals for West Ham, making me the top marksman at the club. Remember, both Geoff Hurst and Pop Robson were at the club at the time. I didn't miss a single Cup or League game. In the League Cup run, I hit the net on four occasions. Stoke City beat us over a four-game semi-final (two legs and two replays). Bobby [Moore] *had to go in goal during the last leg of that tie after Bobby Ferguson went off, but he asked me to do it at first. I was nervous and still quite young and I wanted to try and score a goal to put the side into the Final. The pitch was terrible, a lot of them were, including Upton Park, but Old Trafford was a mud patch that night. Everyone was just slipping and sliding. I did go in goal against Leeds. I was more mature and sure of myself and I put myself forward to take over from Fergie* [Bobby Ferguson].

'Whenever I went on the soccer field, I wanted to play. One of the best games was that first League Cup game at Stoke. I scored with a volley, beating Gordon Banks - that

*was special! Not too many people were able to do that.
There are a few games that stick out in your mind, but
Geoff Hurst couldn't beat Banks from the penalty spot in
the second leg at Upton Park and that's the way it goes...
that's soccer. That defeat meant that I missed out on
becoming one of the first black players to be involved in a
major Wembley final.*

*'That happened again in 1975, but this time it was John
Lyall that blocked the way. Missing the FA Cup in '75 was
what made me leave West Ham. I wanted to help the club
win the Cup so badly. Not to be involved hurt me.
Everything was resolved later, but it affected our
relationship. I'd played in the fourth round against
Swindon. I love Patsy Holland; I made the goal he scored in
the replay at Upton Park. If anybody is going to be in the
Cup Final, I want Patsy to be there. But, when John Lyall
put Bobby Gould in the side before me, I'm saying, "What's
going on?" I said, "Hey, that's it!" I think Ron Greenwood –
although John Lyall was the team manager at the time –
pressed to have me on and Gould as sub. There weren't
really any agents in those days, the way there are now.
Managers didn't alter the way they'd always done things.
Now, there wouldn't be such a problem. I wasn't going to
stay and put up with that! To me, that wasn't fair. Bobby
Gould is not what I call a players' player. The crowd thought
I was far better, too! That was the straw that broke the
camel's back and I said, "Hey, I'm out of here." But that's
soccer, and you have to be big enough to come through it
and I think I came through it pretty good.*

'Hey, those sorts of things happen. Up to this day, I still think John made a mistake, but he was the boss. I had to live with it. But I'm not the type to be content to be a squad player, as so many players seem to be in the modern game. I couldn't just take the money.

'When Hurst went to Stoke, West Ham let him go too early. I think the idea was for me to take his place, being the target man and holding up the ball. Fine, but, if they had kept Geoff on for a while, I was a young player and could have learned a lot from him. At the same time, defenders worrying about Hurst gave me space. But I learned a lot from Pop Robson. He was a nice guy; a modest man. West Ham were a running, gunning side, but we started to play better defensively. Of course, Ted McDougall came but he didn't fit with the kind of patient build-up tactics we worked on. He wanted long balls aimed at him.

'Roger Cross might have been bigger at the club but I suppose Geoff and myself kept him out of the team. Like Pop, he understood how things were done at Upton Park, how we liked to play the game – the "West Ham way". Keith Miller could have done well if Bobby [Moore] hadn't been around. But, as is the case with the rest of life, in football it's about being in the right place at the right time.

'I would like to take Bermudan football as far as possible. It's difficult when you're dealing with the amateur world against the professional world. There are very good players in the amateur world; they need to have the same opportunities as the professionals. At times, you might find one or two better players, but money plays a big part. You

113

have to have money to be able to give your kids exposure and let them play games.

'We can take inspiration from Jamaica and Haiti. They have demonstrated that Caribbean teams could make it to the World Cup Finals. Our kids do have a passion, and to play football in the first place you've got to have character. If you don't have character, you're not going to be a decent soccer player. By bringing them to England, that's what we're hoping. It will make them understand. I tell them, "Hey, where you come from, it's different. You've got to come here and you've got to make adjustments." The thing I'd stress to them is that, when you're in Rome, you do as the Romans do. You don't come to a person's country and expect it to be like home. You're coming here, you gotta make the most of it.'

When Clyde pursued the US soccer dream, he joined the team that encapsulated the razzmatazz of the land of the free more than any other. The Tampa Bay Rowdies, based in Tampa, Florida, was founded as a NASL expansion franchise in 1975 by George Strawbridge. The team turned out for ten seasons at Tampa Stadium and won their single Soccer Bowl Championship in their first season, beating the Portland Timbers 2-0. The Rowdies were defeated in the finals in 1978 and 1979.

In their time, the Rowdies recruited players to their ranks such as midfield captain Rodney Marsh (Queen's Park Rangers, Manchester City and Fulham). They were guided by some of the best young talent who had honed their skills in the English game, such as Eddie Firmani and Gordon Jago.

As a side, they certainly had a knack for making things happen, being an innovative and exciting team. The Rowdies' supporters were known as 'Fannies' (a play on the word 'fan'). The most famous Fannies were the 'North End Zone Gang', also referred to as the 'Ozone', the 'Yellow Card Section', the 'Mooners' and the 'Village Idiots'. The group were made up of college-aged, beer-drinking males and were notorious for their outlandish behaviour that included flinging dead mullets dressed in mini Fort Lauderdale Strikers kits on to the pitch. Of all the American fan groups, the Fannies most approximated the more chaotic fan groups based in England, Germany, Italy and Holland.

The Rowdies also had an indoor soccer team from 1975 to 1984, playing at Bayfront Center Arena in St Petersburg, Florida, and were twice crowned Champions in 1976 and 1980.

After the 1983 season, the Rowdies were sold to Stella Thayer, Bob Blanchard and Dick Corbett. But, following the downfall of the NASL in 1984, Cornelia Corbett became sole owner of the team. Rodney Marsh took over as coach as the Rowdies operated as an independent team for two years, before becoming part of the American Indoor Soccer Association for a single season (1986/87).

In the summer of 1988, the Rowdies joined the third manifestation of the American Soccer League. They would remain with this league and its successor, the APSL (American Professional Soccer League), until they ceased trading following the 1993 season. Notable honours include winning the NASL Championships in 1975, and various division titles in 1975, 1976, 1978, 1979 and 1980.

When not plying his trade in the US, Clyde added to his experience and skills by playing in the Netherlands, a country that had become a sort of football Mecca after the nation's apparent mastery of the 'total football' concept. Clyde remembers:

'I played in Holland, which was very good for me. I use a lot of that experience in my coaching. The Dutch have a real feeling for developing young players and not ruining them with over-coaching and "too much, too soon". In Holland, every kid is treated like an individual, not as an "age-type" and they get to play in every position, for fun, but also to get a feel for the whole game. I've known people to go from being a kid to retirement never having played in more than one position; that is a kind of purposeful ignorance; there's no need for it. It is not healthy in any way.

'I spent the summer of 1976 playing in the North American Soccer League for the Tampa Bay Rowdies. With Tamp, I won the Championship in my first year. I played with the likes of Johnny Sissons, some great players. Tampa were the only side able to give the Cosmos team a run for their money. They had Pelé.

'I was back in Europe for the 1977/78 season, playing for Feyenoord. This was a good move as far as building for the future was concerned. Holland was very good. I learned a lot there, and it has stood me in good stead over the years. It was a terrifically technical league and it was great coming across the likes of Wim Jansen, Ruud

116

Krol and Ari Haan. If we were to emulate them in this country, it would make us better. Holland was fantastic. If I were to play today, I'd play over there. They give you a good background. But, in 1978, I decided to settle in America full-time.

'I moved to Portland Timbers and, for a time, played in the same side as Clive Charles. I also played for Toronto Blizzard.'

The first incarnation of the Blizzard were Toronto Metros. This team made its NASL debut in 1971 bringing First Division soccer back to Toronto after a three-year break following the demise of the Toronto Falcons. The Varsity Stadium was home to the Metros, and one of the side's leading players was Dick Howard, formally of Chester.

The franchise merged with Toronto Croatia of the National Soccer League in 1975 to create Toronto Metros-Croatia and included some big names, such as Eusébio, in their line-up and, in 1976, won the NASL Championship.

The Toronto Blizzard came into being after the Global Television Network bought the floundering Toronto Metros-Croatia on 1 February 1979. Following the purchase, Toronto Croatia returned to the NSL.

The Blizzard were part of the NASL between 1979 and 1984 (the final year of the league's existence). They were runners-up in the League Championship in 1983 and, in the playoff final, before a crowd of almost 60,000, were defeated 2–0 in the Soccer Bowl by the Tulsa Roughnecks in the BC Place Stadium, Vancouver. They lost again in 1984, this time to the Chicago Sting, two games to nil in a best-of-three Championship series. The squad included the likes of Roberto Bettega, formally of Juventus (between 1968 and 1983 he played 326 games for 'the Old Lady', scoring 199 goals). He turned out for the Italian national team 42 times (1975-83), netting 19 times for Le Azzurri. Jimmy Nicholl was also a Blizzard during the same period. The Canadian-born (Hamilton, Ontario) Northern Irish International had played for Manchester United and Sunderland and would return to the UK to wear the blue of Glasgow Rangers for 106 games and later join West Bromwich Albion. Nicholl is currently the assistant manager of Aberdeen, working with Jimmy Calderwood.

Blizzard got to the playoffs in 1979 and 1982, losing in the first round both times. During the first four years of the club's existence, the playing staff included Clyde Best, Jim Bone (Norwich City, Sheffield United, Partick Thistle), Jimmy Greenhoff (Leeds United, Birmingham City, Stoke City, Manchester United, Crewe Alexandra and Port Vale – he returned to England to play for Rochdale in 1981), Peter Lorimer (Leeds United, York City) and David Fairclough (Liverpool, Norwich City, Lucerne, Oldham Athletic, Tranmere Rovers, SK Beveren and Wigan Athletic).

In 1985, not a year after the Toronto Blizzard concluded operations after the NASL folded, the owners, York-Hanover, bought out the Ontario-based Dynamo Latino (established 1922) from the semi-professional National Soccer League. The intention was to call them the Toronto Blizzard. Although NSL rules did not permit alterations to club names in the middle of a season, in 1986 Toronto Blizzard were included in the NSL.

Under former assistant coach Dave Turner, the club won the League Championship and the NSL Cup, while Toronto Italia won the Playoff Championship. The Blizzard roster featured former NASL stars Paul Hammond, Randy Ragan and Paul James. The Blizzard played just the single campaign in the NSL before joining the newly formed Canadian Soccer League in 1987.

Although finishing the regular season on top of the CSL's Eastern Division, in 1990 the Blizzard were knocked out in the first round of the playoffs. In 1991, the team were defeated in the Championship Final by the Vancouver 86ers, despite a couple of remarkable long-range goals by Canadian international Branko Segota. It was the 86ers' fourth consecutive League Championship. The CSL embodiment of the Blizzard included Paul Peschisolido, who would be sold to Birmingham City (the first of eleven English clubs he would play for up to 2007) at the conclusion of the 1993 season.

The CSL disappeared after the 1993 season after the Toronto Blizzard and Vancouver 86ers walked out on the league to become part of the American Professional Soccer League (which had shrunk to just four franchises) and returned to their former NASL home ground at the University of Toronto's Varsity Stadium. But, with a quarter of the season remaining, financial difficulties and poor attendance figures obliged the team to move on to the Lamport Stadium, which was owned by the city of Toronto.

That year, the Blizzard ended up fifth in the league with 10 victories and 14 defeats and, as such, failed to make the playoffs. Karsten Von Wersebe, the Blizzard owner, had taken the club from the CSL to the APSL, hoping that the league would be given American Division One status, as FIFA had instructed that a national Division One-quality soccer league should be generated in the USA as a condition of America being awarded the World Cup in 1994. But the US Soccer Federation made the decision to create a new league, Major League Soccer, so delivering what was to be a killer punch to the floundering Blizzard and Von Wersebe at the end of the 1993 term.

In 2001, the proposal to form a Canadian United Soccer League and the Toronto Blizzard (with a new consortium of owners) were reported to be interested in a franchise. When the idea of the CUSL died, the return of the Blizzard looked less than unlikely. But when Toronto were given a Major League Soccer franchise in 2005, there was some speculation that the team would be given the Blizzard name; however, in the end, Toronto FC came into being and, with that, the Blizzard were consigned to the vaults of North American soccer history.

Following his stay in Canada, Best moved on to indoor soccer:

'I played indoors with Los Angeles Lazers; Clive was there, too. I hung up my boots in 1984, but I did some coaching, school football, at Woodbridge High – that's where US international Joe-Max Moore came from – and the professional indoor side San Diego Sockers. Although it made financial sense, the NASL didn't provide me with

enough stimulation. The USA was good, but it was easy for me. It wasn't much of a challenge. You could play with your eyes closed. So I set up a dry-cleaning business in California, but football was in my blood and, late in 1997, I took on the challenge of running the Bermudan side. My first game in charge resulted in a 2–1 victory over St Martin.

'I was shocked to find, when speaking to people in England, that players don't come back in the afternoon. That is amazing. When I'm paying you £100,000 a week for playing and you're not going to come back in the afternoon, something's wrong. When you see what players are getting today, our pay wasn't good. But, compared to the people that played before us, and the average man on the street, it was excellent. We played a part in what players get today. You can't complain, you never look back, you don't envy anyone, you get paid for the job... we did it to the best of our ability, and it was fun while we did it. Money's nice to have, but it's nothing, if you've got your health.

'When I look at Geoff Hurst, he's definitely one of the best centre-forwards I've seen in my life. I look at Trevor [Brooking] over the years... after I'd long gone, he developed into one of the best midfield players in the world. One person that I would definitely put on my sheet first if I were picking a West Ham team would be Billy Bonds. Billy had the heart of a lion; he never knew when to quit. You'd always put him in your side; he'd give nothing less than 100 per cent

'Shortly after passing my driving test, I picked up Billy,

giving him a lift to West Ham's training ground. Just past Canning Town flyover, an articulated lorry made a U-turn right in front of us, blocking the road. Billy thought we were going to go right under the thing. I was just staring at the blockage ahead, slowly sinking in my seat. The lorry completed its turn with a split-second to spare, but I lost control and the car bounced along the central reservation. We got to Chadwell Heath, but spent most of the morning recovering from the journey.

'Bobby Moore will always stick out in my mind; he had it all. Grace on the field, a good passer of the ball, good mentality. Bobby was a giant of international football, but he was an ordinary person, he had time for everybody. He was a great man and great friend. If he hadn't been a great player, he would still have been a great man anyway. When you had problems, you could always pull him aside and ask him for advice and he'd always give it. He was the best player in the world. I saw Franz Beckenbauer play and Bobby was better than him. You play soccer with your brain, and Bobby beat everyone in that department. He never played any differently, whether on a match day, practice matches or in training… he concentrated as if playing in a World Cup Final. I am so grateful to have played with him. I have been able to achieve what I have because of him. Bobby Moore was the best player ever.

'People talk about who is the greatest player in terms of skill. Trevor Brooking would be in the frame, but I'd always say Bobby Moore; I know precisely what I would get from him. Then there was Geoff Hurst and Martin Peters, Pop

Robson and Patsy Holland – they were excellent players.

'All the players I played with at West Ham had qualities. We all played different positions. We had tons of players. I remember a little feller called Stevie Lane; he was in the youth team with me. He never quite made it, he didn't have the temperament. Ability-wise, he was one of the best wingers I've seen in my life, but he didn't have the right attitude. People like Bob Glosier and Keith Miller never made it, but could have if the breaks had gone their way. We had so many good players who would have made it in any other outfit. It was a privilege to be playing in the First Division. You're playing with quality players week in and week out. There were ups and downs, but that's life in general. It's being able to weigh the good times against the bad times and see where you go from there.

'You have ups and downs in soccer. The person who comes through the downs is the one able to get where they want to be. It's difficult. I just wish we would have won more because that's what you want. It's all right playing attractive football, it's great, but at the end of the day you want some silverware. We didn't quite achieve that. The reason we didn't was the style of soccer we played. It was open, attacking soccer. To be realistic, you're not going to win things like that in the long run. You've got to be organised, you've got to be smart, but the way we played was the way you like to play and, from the spectators' point of view, it's great to watch. I enjoyed it, but I just wish we had won more trophies.

'It's good to get off the island from time to time. It is

beautiful but a bit small. I have to come away and air myself – that's why I'm glad I'm on this trip. Now I can go back and rejuvenate, start all over. The mother of one of the lads I brought over talked to the Bermudan press about the passion these boys have for the game and her belief that the experience would develop the character of these young men. That's my task, why I have brought them to Upton Park.

'The fans at West Ham, in a sense, are like the fans at any other place; when you're playing well, they're with you... when you're not playing too good, they let you know, because the crowd were so close to the pitch at Upton Park you tended to hear a bit more, but they were very knowledgeable. They knew what they wanted. Winning wasn't an end in itself. They just wanted to see attractive soccer. It was our responsibility to try to give them that and I think that we were very successful in that respect. We played very good soccer.

'I'll never forget those memories of England. For me, at the time, West Ham was just the best place in the world with the best people. They made me feel welcome and at home, which, given the differences between the East End and Bermuda, is quite an achievement. I loved my time there.

'At Upton Park on 20 September 1975, I came on to replace Alan Taylor as substitute and scored a goal. It was my first appearance of the season. Sheffield United were the visitors. My header came off the upright, but I stabbed the ball past Jim Brown on the rebound. He was a good 'keeper. Tommy Taylor, our centre-half, who was manager at Orient

for a time, scored as well. That was to be my final goal at Upton Park. Four days later, in the second-round League Cup replay against Bristol City, I scored my last goal for the club, helping them into the next round. I got a handful of games before the end of 1975.

'In mid-January 1976, I was again brought off of the substitutes' bench to replace Alan Taylor in a 3-0 defeat at Maine Road. This was not the way I would have wanted to end my relationship with West Ham, but I was never again to play for the club.

'But, by 1976, I wanted to get away from West Ham. When you've been in the first team and you don't see yourself making progress, it's up and down, you don't want that. The time was right. I did the right thing. I probably should have stayed and played in England a lot longer. I know I would have reached the heights that I probably should have. I didn't lack the fundamental ability. At the time, you saw things getting on your nerves, saw things going the wrong way. What really annoyed me was that I was looking at a player like Bobby Gould getting in the team every week. Bill Shankly was right when he said the guy couldn't trap a bag of cement. I'm sitting on the bench, saying to myself, "Hey! That don't make sense to me. So I might as well look somewhere else and play."

'I wasn't happy at the time but you can't spend the rest of your life being bitter. If I had my time over again, I would still go back to West Ham; when I come back to England, I always go back to Upton Park. I've got claret-and-blue blood in my veins!

'I didn't see myself as a pioneer. At the time, it was a job. In later years, I learned that people looked up to you for making it into the side, but, now that I look back, I think, Hey! If I made people happy by doing that, if I paved the way, I just have to thank the Lord for giving me the opportunity to do that. I didn't set out with the intentions of being a pioneer, being the first or the second. I just wanted to play soccer. West Ham was the only place I could do that.

'I never saw racism at West Ham. At times, playing away, especially up north, someone would shout "nigger" from the terraces, but you've got to be mentally strong – ignore them. As a professional, you had to block it out. For my team-mates, the West Ham fans, the people that mattered to me, race was never an issue. You had to carry yourself in the right manner. Show them the soccer ball doesn't care what colour you are. Give your answer by sticking one in the back of their net.

'There was one game, at Goodison, at the start of the 1970s, I was getting some stick from their fans, racist stuff, but I got the ball just on the halfway line. I beat a string of defenders before scoring and, from that point on, the Everton crowd respected me. The best way to counter that sort of thing is to play well, score – give it right back to 'em!

'But it would not be right to just think of myself. There were people supporting me. But now, when there are racist incidents, like there have been in Europe, the authorities – FIFA, UEFA – need to show a responsible attitude. In England, the problem seems to have been sorted out, but in other parts of the world help is needed. This day and age, *something needs to be done. If necessary, close the stadiums, get them where it hurts – in the wallet. But, also, players need to take responsibility, too... not be intimidated and say when things are happening, if only for the sake of the next generation of players.*

'At the time I was playing, it was just a job to me. But, a couple of years ago, I went to a dinner celebrating black players in England, where I was introduced as "the legend" and lads like Cyrille Regis and Luther Blissett shook my hand and told me how I'd been their inspiration. When I see black kids playing in England and think maybe I played a part in their emergence, that's my satisfaction.

'Someone had to be the first. Maybe it was God's plan and He selected me for the job. I wanted to play football and do well, but I did think of those coming after me, not just myself. Things have changed today... if I had anything to do with that, that's great. That's what I would have wanted to do.

'Racism existed then, that can't be denied, but those problems didn't happen at Upton Park, apart from a few stupid people. You could have run away from it, go home, but that wasn't me. I get asked, "How did you tolerate it?" I say that I understood that I had a responsibility to set an example for black kids everywhere. I did it to the best I could, and I did pretty well, I think.

'Bobby [Moore] took abuse wherever he went... that had nothing to do with the colour of his skin but because he was good at stopping the other team. Bobby taught me that

it does no good hiding; you have to get out there and do your job – focus, concentrate and get on with what needs doing. If you let people get into your head, they are going to steal your game from you. You mustn't allow that to happen. You keep your game yours.

'Being around Bobby week in and week out, I got support; he was always there and always brave and sensible. He wanted the best for you and he was a fantastic person. He kept himself under control and I learned to do that from him; don't lose it, stay with what you have to do. You never saw things get the better of him, and I tried to emulate him in that respect. Being in his company taught you how to handle anything that came your way.

'There was never racism in our dressing room. We didn't look at things that way, black or white – we were all mates. If it was ever at West Ham, I haven't seen it. If I were to come across racism anywhere, I would say to the people, "It's time you woke up, it's the 21st century. Let's face it, we've all got to live together." But it was true that clubs in England were anxious about giving black players a chance at the time I arrived. Eusébio and Pelé and other black players had proved themselves to be among the best in the world, but black players didn't get the same chances in the Football League as they do now. The old idea that black players have "rhythm" is true, but we didn't even get recognised for that in the late 1960s. In football, or anything else, a person should be judged by their ability and not their colour. When you score a goal, no one looks at your colour. That's a great thing about soccer.

'East London continues to feel like home – or home from home, maybe. I miss the place and the comradeship of football.'

As Clyde scrambled out of the rain behind the wheel of the Bermudan Football Association minibus – although being team-bus driver was not part of his contract – he was unable to conceal his longing for the simplicity and joy of his earlier career, and the pain of the politics and manoeuvrings that characterise his more recent involvement in the game.

Coming towards the end of his time as his country's soccer leader, Best, a Bermudan sporting hero, found himself caught in a tangle of envy, conspiracy and disloyalty, which eventually led to government intervention. Two days before Christmas 2000, Clyde was summoned to the headquarters of the Bermuda FA by the organisation's president, Neville Tyrrell. Best was told his contract would not be renewed at the end of the month. Neither he nor the public was told why; few people who cared were less than astonished. He had not yet served three years, nowhere near enough time to turn a nation's footballing fortunes around, but there was no conceivable way he could be seen to have failed.

The island's daily newspaper, the *Royal Gazette*, asked why 'a man whose silky skills during his West Ham heyday did more to put this country on the map than any number of politicians' ambassadorial trips overseas' should have been treated so poorly, when he had so successfully restored the credibility of his country's football.

A source within the Bermuda FA was quoted as being

129

disgusted with what they felt was a 'witch-hunt' against Best, and documents were 'leaked' demonstrating how the FA's coaching committee had been making plans to replace Best with a 'big-name consultant' because Best was supposedly not 'enlivening' the public.

But Clyde's record has been good and a national radio debate polled 99 per cent support for Best. For all this, the former Hammer found that his island home had changed while he had been away. It was dominated by financial considerations, while young people did not seem as prepared as they had once been to listen and learn. The young were now affluent, well travelled and more of them hankered after basketball in the United States than football in England. This was a generation to whom the name of Clyde Best meant little.

But most over the age of 30 in Bermuda know Clyde. Wherever he goes, waves and smiles mark his route. When he drove the FA bus down the pastel-tinted avenues of the island, even his opponents found it difficult not to like the modest and honest Best. Bermudians have never been great respecters of status. It is said that David Bowie, who has a home on the island, can stroll along Hamilton's Front Street and nobody takes as much as a second glance. Yet, according to Clyde, sometimes it can be a 'suffocating place'. He wondered if small-island jealousies had conspired against him. He had been voted out by a coaching committee of unpaid officials, who, for Best, had no concept of what is needed to produce an international football team and Tyrrell barely ever spoke to him.

Best was trying to develop a professional attitude, but, before the game with BVI had kicked off, he was running around sorting out crises, not so much as technical director but more as bus driver, nurse, courier, administrator and motivator. A player had forgotten his passport, which the FIFA official wanted to see as proof of his eligibility to play; and Clyde had to delegate someone to retrieve it from the hotel. Then he was trying to find a jersey for his goalkeeper as an official was not happy about the colour of the one the player was wearing.

'This stuff drives you batty,' he mumbled. By the time he had gone into the traditional cluster with his side for a collective recital of the 'Lord's Prayer', he already felt exhausted. He now had to deal with the notoriously demanding crowd, including a collection of envious coaches.

He groaned that he knew how Kevin Keegan felt, and exclaimed that, even if his side were playing Brazil, the crowd would still expect Bermuda to win. He wasn't far wrong; as the ninth goal went in, there were complaints that it wasn't 15.

After the game, Dennis Lister, Bermuda's sports minister, told how he grew up watching and admiring Best and confirmed that there was a sentiment strongly felt in the community that the FA's decision needed to be reassessed. He talked to both Best and the FA about negotiating some form of rethink. Clyde was philosophical, reflecting on how funny it was that, in England, he had never been treated the way he had been by some of the football people in Bermuda. He talked exasperatedly of how the new government of the island wanted to 'Bermudianise' the nation, yet other

Bermudians just wanted to kick one of their own in the pants. He said, 'You know, this is my home and it will always be home. I've no regrets about coming back; it enabled me to spend some quality time with my dad before he died… but, if I could, I'd probably go back to England tomorrow.'

Clyde buttoned up his coat and pulled on his baseball cap to protect against the biting wind. Maybe there was something about his experience in the latter days of his time in charge of his nation's team which reminded him of the verbal poison he endured as the Hammers roamed the icy hinterland of football racism. He was able to treat that with the contempt it deserved by way of courage and the stoic support of his claret-and-blue team-mates. Perhaps recalling how he was admired all those years ago in London's East End, he felt more appreciated on the cold days at the Boleyn Ground than by the flawless beaches of paradise. A hero warrants something better.

Clyde had probably been a bigger star in America than he had in Britain. His record in the USA was one of the best during the early years of the modern game there:

NASL REGULAR SEASON AND PLAYOFFS

	Regular Season			Playoffs		
	GP	G	A	GP	G	A
1975 Tampa Bay Rowdies	19	6	5	3	2	1
1976 Tampa Bay Rowdies	19	9	6	2	0	0
1977 Portland Timbers	25	7	4	-	-	-
1978 Portland Timbers	30	12	9	5	2	0
1979 Portland Timbers	29	8	8	-	-	-
1980 Portland Timbers	30	11	6	-	-	-
1981 Portland Timbers	4	0	0	-	-	-
1981 Toronto Blizzard	19	1	4	-	-	-
1982 Toronto Blizzard	3	1	1	-	-	-
Total	**178**	**55**	**43**	**10**	**4**	**1**

GP = Games Played   G = Goals   A = Assists

In 2004, Clyde was inducted into the Bermuda National Sports Hall of Fame. During the Bermuda Football Association Annual Congress Meeting on Thursday, 16 September 2004, Clyde was presented with the FIFA Order of Merit.

In recent years, Clyde has been involved with the Westgate Correction Centre Bermuda, a place he has had a long association with since working there as an officer. He recently said that, although unlawful killing isn't a big problem on the island, drugs posed a challenge to the community and it is part of his work to become involved with inmates prior to their release with the aim of sending them back into society as 'better people', less likely to reoffend. According to Clyde, he treats 'people as I would want to be treated', and talking to individuals about football is a 'way in'. The fact that many of the people whom Clyde works with do not reoffend gives him tremendous satisfaction.

Most recently, he has worked in a transitional centre for prison inmates (Bermuda has the fifth-highest prison population in the world), advising those who are ready to be released back into society.

He was awarded an MBE in the January 2006 New Year's Honours list for services to football and the community in Bermuda. He found out via a simple phone call while he was at work. He felt it to be a great honour, but also incredible that he should get such an accolade for doing something he loved, so long ago. One of his first thoughts was that – along with Bobby Moore, Geoff Hurst, Martin Peters, Trevor Brooking and others – West Ham had possibly achieved some sort of record in terms of getting what amounted to official national recognition. His reaction was typical of his modesty and gentlemanliness, seeing it as being an honour to be bracketed with Bobby Moore, Sir Geoff Hurst and Sir Bobby Charlton, and he expressed thanks to West Ham for 'the opportunity to... make people happy'.

He also saw the part his upbringing played in his achievements. Although his parents have passed away, he was sure they would be very proud. His father had received an MBE for his work in the prison service, and Clyde was pleased to have emulated his dad.

For all this, Best might have received recognition earlier. It would have certainly had more impact on the nature of racism in society if he had been honoured closer to the end of his playing career in England. However, it may have been that playing exhibition games in South Africa under the Apartheid regime went against him. But, as both Bobby Moore and Johnny Byrne had challenged racism in South Africa by their footballing activity there, Clyde had taken part more with the aim of breaking barriers than reinforcing them. But many saw him as selling out and there are not a few commentators, especially in the Caribbean, who think that, maybe if he hadn't made that trip, we might be talking about 'Sir Clyde Best' now.

Best has maintained a strong interest in his nation's involvement in football, recently letting off a string of attacks against the Bermuda Football Association for what he saw as the wretched state of the domestic game, including the lack of regular matches for the national team and for not hiring a full-time development officer who would be responsible for lobbying the corporate world for extra funding and sponsorship. Following Bermuda's 3-0 defeat by New England Revolution, the island's first international game for eight months, Best argued that Bermuda would stand no chance of being consistently competitive at international tournaments unless the national team played and trained together on a more regular basis.

But Clyde remains a Hammer and keeps up with the current state of play at Upton Park. He admired Alan Pardew and feels he did a good job. Clyde watched Pardew's Hammers play against Fulham in the second half of the 2005/06 season and approved of the way the side equipped themselves. He saw the Irons' two goals as 'the goals of the year' and believed Anton Ferdinand and Yossi Benayoun (who has since moved to Liverpool) to be class performers, with a style that suited the traditions of West Ham. Of course, he

135

recalls West Ham's current manager, Alan Curbishley, as a young player, who broke into the Hammers first team in the latter part of Clyde's time at the club (they actually played together four times in the first team in the 1974/75 season) and he has a high regard for the man once known by players and fans at Upton Park as 'Whiz'.

Talking early in 2007 about the new regime at Upton Park, he said, 'For anybody to come in and just take it over would not feel right. You have had generations of people supporting the club, with season tickets passed on through the family. One day, I was sitting in my living room in Bermuda when there was a knock on the door. It was a West Ham supporter who was over from England and just wanted to say hello. That's the sort of club it is.'

Clyde also continues to take an interest in the wider issues relating to football. When asked about the Spanish national coach, Luis Aragones, calling Thierry Henry 'a black shit', Clyde responded without hesitation, 'Hey, show him the door if he makes comments like that. It's inexcusable.'

Some commentators have suggested that Clyde under-achieved, but his impact as the first black footballer to imprint himself on the national consciousness in British football's TV era could never be measured by goals alone.

Looking forward to coming to London to pick up his honour, which he had requested to be bestowed in June 2006 (wanting to wait for the warmer weather), he said, 'I'm looking forward to coming back to visit Buckingham Palace. I'm sure my wife and daughter will want to come over, too. It'll be nice to meet up with some old friends and have a good knees-up.'

6

CLIVE MICHAEL CHARLES

'Clive Charles was a very well-balanced full-back. He was very graceful, particularly for a defender. He started out as a midfielder, of course, but he converted to a modern attacking left-back and was able to do a great job in that role. He struck me as a very intelligent and thoughtful young man. He seemed to want to learn. He was totally different as far as football went from his brother John, even though they played in the same position. But I think, looking back, that Clive was always going to make a very good coach. He took the most out of being at West Ham with Bobby Moore and then, of course, he worked for a time with Frank O'Farrell. I think he learned from those experiences but also developed his own way of doing things.'

RON GREENWOOD – WEST HAM AND ENGLAND

'I saw Clive as our key to some kind of success and I wanted to build a team round him at Cardiff. He was a natural leader and a very bright man. He was also a great guy to have on your team, able to pick people up when they were down and get them to look forward. He always wanted to do things better. He didn't dwell on mistakes and failures, only in as much as seeing how what went wrong could help make the team stronger for the next match.'

FRANK O'FARRELL – FORMER MANAGER OF CARDIFF CITY,

LEICESTER CITY AND MANCHESTER UNITED

'Charles was a good captain... the kind of man you want on the pitch leading your team. You could work with Clive, you see, he could listen and he wanted to understand, which is half the job done for a manager. He was also skilful for a full-back at that time and a good example to younger players later on. He was good with bringing people into the game.'

JIMMY ANDREWS – FORMER MANAGER OF CARDIFF CITY

'Clive was a great player... I really mean that. I know he's my little brother and all, but he always tried to learn off others. He's also a great manager. Look what he's done in the States. I couldn't do that, I don't have the patience. But he has kind of taught himself to have patience. Takes some doing, that.'

JOHN CHARLES – WEST HAM UNITED

The youngest of nine children, Clive was the brother of John Charles, West Ham United's first black player. The Charleses were one of only six sets of brothers to play League football for West Ham.

Many European players migrated to the USA in the early 1970s, but Clive Charles was one of the few who stayed after the financial collapse of soccer in North America. He helped to build a structure from the grass roots to work with players who went on to play for the national teams of Canada, Mexico and the United States, and populate the professional ranks in America, Europe and Asia. Those he worked with won Olympic gold medals, and were victorious in World Cup football; many of these people, touched by Clive's example, went on to become teachers of football themselves.

Clive can be considered one of the real pioneers and champions of the modern game in America. His biography is a rags-to-riches story if ever there was one. If ever one needed to demonstrate that human talent will overcome adversity, look to Clive Charles.

I contacted Clive at his home in Maine, USA, and he offered the following reflections on his career with West Ham and beyond.

'I played my first game for the West Ham first team on 21 March 1972; it was a 1–1 draw at Highfield Road. It was on the same night that Frank Lampard played for England against Yugoslavia; that's why I got a game. I was lucky enough to help create the goal that gave West Ham the draw. There were about ten minutes of the first half to go

when I crossed to Pat Holland, who headed it down for Clyde [Best] to put it past Bill Glazier, the Coventry 'keeper. I got three more League games that season.

'I played in the game against Tottenham Hotspur on 1 April 1972 - April Fool's day! That was first time three black players had played on the same side in the First Division. But probably more significant for us, after Kevin Lock came on as substitute for Johnny Ayris, Kevin laid on Ade Coker's goal; the average age of the 11 players on the field was just 21 at that point.

'I was born in Bow, East London, on 3 October 1951 and went straight to West Ham from school, having been associated with the club from the age of 12. I'd been going to the Tuesday and Thursday training evenings at the club. West Ham was always my club. My school days were spent in Canning Town and a couple of teachers were helpful.

'I first noticed that I had some talent for football at the age of eight. Albert Dunlop, a teacher at my first school, Star Lane, and David Jones at Pretoria, they were both helpful to me, but they didn't coach you in those days. My first real coach was John Lyall at West Ham. He was a wonderful teacher, a natural. We were very much on the same wavelength. He looked at the game intelligently and had a way of reading people. He had a real philosophy and, although the club meant everything to him, he always did what he saw as right for a player. I admired him for that and took a lot of his ways into my own coaching. He had a lot of patience but the one thing he didn't like was

people who'd suck up to him. He'd sooner people be polite and respectful than give him a load of flannel.

'*I was good at cricket. I played for Newham and London Boys, but it was something I played in the summer; it was never going to compete with football. I was approached by some people from Essex to go down to Chelmsford, but I wasn't ever going to take it up. I kind of knew my future would be in football.*

'*I was the last of nine children, all different colours! There was Jessie, Josie, Bon, Len, Bonzo, Marge, Rita and John. Another died. John was the next eldest and seven years older than me. The first four were white, as was Michael, who died. Then there was Bonzo and Margie – they were sort of like me... tanned! My mum, Jessie, she was a housewife. I wouldn't say the family was poor, not compared to some others around us. We never went short of anything that mattered, but I suppose we didn't want a lot. But, compared to some, we didn't have much in the way of material things and you had to work hard to get by in the East End at that time. You had to keep going.*

'*As you know, coming from the area yourself, Plaistow, Canning Town and that district have always been thought of as deprived areas, and they were and are. Some people had a hard time of it and, yes, life was never easy there, but we had a lot of fun as well. But, when you think back, from where I am now, you think, Wow! We did OK! I certainly think that a lot of people here in America would see Canning Town in the late Fifties and early Sixties as quite a tough place to make something of yourself. But, there are worse places.*

'When I was still living in my family home in Canning Town, Clyde [Best] lived with us, so he was like a brother. I'm still close to my family back in London – John, my brother, his wife Carol and their kids and grandkids. My mum, 50 years ago in Canning Town, could never have dreamed that her sons and grandchildren would have achieved so much.

'My brother John did a good job of not spending any time with me. But that probably helped. It allowed me to develop my own style. I was a totally different player to John. He was a hard, tough-tackling player. I was more of a footballer. I liked to get forward on the overlap. As such, it wasn't too long before I attracted the interest of the England Youth set-up. I got four Youth caps and played alongside John McDowell.

'Getting into the England Youth side showed that I was good in my own right; it wasn't just about my brother being in the team. We never actually played together in the first team for West Ham, but we did play in the same Football Combination side during most of the 1970/71 season. I think I was a good player, but it wasn't like now; there was not a shortage of left-sided defenders then, at least not to the extent there is in the current English game. I was potentially on a par with most of the people who could play at left-back at Upton Park; it was just that they had become established before I matured. I'm not bitter about that, it is the way football is. Like a lot of things in life, you have to make the most of what you've got, and that's what I had at West Ham.

'I signed pro forms in 1968. By the time I broke into the first-team squad, I was a creative left-back, one of the forerunners of today's wing-backs. However, this wasn't always the case; I was originally a left-centre midfielder. West Ham converted me to a left-back when I was about 15. Most of my games as a colt had been as a midfielder. The problem was that, at the time, I was one of four players fighting for a full-back slot. I was competing against Billy Bonds, Frank Lampard and John McDowell at first. I was close to Frank Lampard. Frank took me under his wing a bit when I came to West Ham. Like me, he had been at Star Lane School and was in the fourth year at Pretoria when I was in my first year.

'Later on, things got a little less cramped. Bill was pushed into midfield, opening up the right-back spot for John McDowell. Nevertheless, I was still understudying McDowell and Lampard, two contenders for the English international defence. There's a time when it's right for you to come into the first team, a moment when you can blossom. Miss that, and it gets harder to make your mark. John [McDowell] was ready to play and I didn't get a chance to establish myself, but that's the way things go in football. Today, at clubs like West Ham, the likes of Frank Lampard and Billy [Bonds] would maybe move on to bigger clubs, clearing the way for younger players to develop, but then, well, players stayed with clubs longer and, unless a young player matured really early, they had to go down a division or two to get regular games. But, effectively, that put you even further down the line in terms

of proving yourself. It was a bit of a gamble, but I can't complain. It's a privilege to do something you love for a living and I had a good crack at that in the English League.

'I've never forgotten my roots and I have fond memories of being at Upton Park. I was friendly with Paul Grotier, Tony Carr and Patsy Holland; we were all in the same youth team together. I remember when we had been beaten 1–0 at Elland Road. Billy Bonds, Ted McDougall and myself were the last players left in the bath. Bonzo had fought for the whole of the game; he had run his balls off. Ted had spent most of the time keeping out of trouble.

'There was an exchange of words then the fists started flying. I was in the middle. I was a young pro and these were big stars! I didn't know what to do. The rest of the team rushed in to pull Bill off Ted. Of course, no one cared about me. I would be out of the team next week. I could have drowned!

'I was with West Ham while Bobby Moore was club captain. Bobby was by far and away the best player I ever played with; no one was even near his class. He was a good passer, but was average at everything else, but put that all together with a unique footballing brain and you got something else.

'I wish I had been more dedicated as a player. They are more dedicated now because of the money. They know what dedication can achieve. I always trained hard, and worked at my game, but we didn't earn much more than a dustman in my day. I was lucky, though. I played against Bobby Charlton, the great Manchester United and Leeds

sides – some good teams. The manager, Ron Greenwood, used to have squads of 24 because we were playing games back to back.

'One Easter, I got a new car; it was second-hand, but it was new to me. I got to the ground late. Normally, it wouldn't matter, I'd only have to get ready to watch the game and, anyway, on that day I was number 24 on a list of 24. But Frank [Lampard, Sr.] had gone sick about an hour before the game and Ron told me I was in… against Spurs, in front of a packed ground.

'We won the match, but I knew I would be out for the next game – that kind of thing was frustrating, it was tough. But I thought, Great! I've got a new car and I get to play against Spurs!

'I played 14 times for the West Ham first team, but I only ever got one clear opportunity to break into the side. It was in the first game of the 1973/74 season. The first game I got in my own right, on the strength of my own form; it was against Newcastle at Upton Park on 25 August 1973. Frank Lampard was playing at right-back and John McDowell had been dropped. It was my chance to stake a claim for a regular place. I'd never had a bad game for West Ham, but we lost that game 1–2 and I had a stinker! I stank the field up – the next game I was out!

'I didn't really know Ron Greenwood; I was a bit young, he was a bit aloof. I learned a lot from him, though, but I learned most from John Lyall. Ron was a great coach… I'm not so sure about him as a man-manager, though. Not a lot of people got close to Ron. I suppose I was a bit intimidated *by him. John Lyall was the first one to make sense. He had something to say, more than "Get forward" or "Stay back". He thought about the game and talked about it in an intelligent way; he articulated his ideas.*

'I don't know if following my brother John to Upton Park was helpful or unhelpful. I think sometimes we expect brothers to be the same, or expect them to be the same way. But everyone was always fair at West Ham.

'In the past, West Ham has been connected with racism – Alf Garnett and all that – but I never experienced any racism at Upton Park. I only really came across it in one game against Manchester United. Ron Greenwood had the balls to take me, Ade Coker and Clyde to Old Trafford. Although Ade didn't play, we took some stick that day. I didn't see myself as paving the way for others when I was playing, but I suppose we must have been. I just didn't think of myself as a black soccer player. I was just earning a living. I've never spoken to today's black players at West Ham so I don't know what they think or how things might have changed. Living 6,000 miles from England, I'm not really qualified to say if blacks are discriminated against in terms of management in England, although I don't see too many black managers. But it's a tight-knit circle, anyway, even in terms of whites. It's the same 20 or so names that get mentioned every time there's a top job going. It's the same in the States in grid-iron and basketball. If Harry [Redknapp] or George Graham got the sack at one club, they'd move on to another. It's a bit of a closed shop anyway.

'As far as West Ham being a racist club is concerned, I can only say that they took me on and I think Ron Greenwood was the first Division One manager to play three black players in the same team. Frank O'Farrell, a former West Ham man, took me to Cardiff and Jimmy Andrews, who had also been at Upton Park, made me club captain at Ninian Park. That was the first time I really thought about the fact that I was a black player. The local newspapers made a big thing about me being the first black player to captain a League side. Until that point, I had thought about myself purely as a footballer rather than a black footballer.

'Yes, problems with race are always a factor and they shouldn't be, but there is a bit of a bandwagon and one or two people make a living out of promoting anti-racism, so it is in their interests to look for and find racism... don't get me wrong, it's there. But I'm not sure how far saying "Don't be racist" gets rid of it. It goes deeper than that. People say racism is about ignorance, and that might be true, but it's more about fear.

'When I was in Canning Town as a kid, we didn't get any noticeable racism, because everyone was more or less on the same level; no one had much of anything. It's when you think you have something to lose to a group of people that you start to dislike that group – that's the bottom line. So, if you are afraid of a group and they happen to be black, you might express that fear and actually become racist. But, if they were just a different religion, you would fear them just as much and discriminate against them just as *much. So if you want to get rid of that sort of thing, you've got to get rid of the fear. And that's not so easy. You can say "Don't be afraid" but that is not going to stop anyone's fear. That won't make them feel less insecure about themselves.*

'You read some stuff that talks about how bad it was or is, but that's the thing to say now; they can't say anything else, really. Just like years ago, they said nothing, often the same people, that was the thing then, you didn't say anything 'cause it was seen as an expected thing. So the people who are saying "This is bad" or "That was bad", you don't know what they are actually thinking, all you know is that they are saying what they have to say now. You are right to stop people shouting out "You black this or that..." but, just because you have stopped them shouting it out, expressing it, it doesn't mean they are OK with race. I suppose it is much harder now to find out who is racist, as anyone who was going to say anything has been educated just not to say it. That stops people being offended, but beyond that, who knows? That has to be done, but it goes deeper than just doing that. Can you make it so that no one ever gets offended about anything? I suppose, if you did, that would have a cost.

'That defeat against Spurs was to be my last game for West Ham. I didn't want to leave Upton Park. The supporters were great; of course, I knew a lot of them. They were always right behind you, even if you had a stinker, they would try to pick you up – "Come on, Charlo!" West Ham is its supporters, really; they make the club. Sometimes that has been forgotten. Growing up in the area, you recognise what

it all means to people. It is kind of central to who people are and I liked that commitment. I've always carried it with me and, in the best of worlds, I'd have got a place in the side and stayed, but I couldn't get in the first team.

'Keith Coleman came from Sunderland, which was going to further limit any prospects. I had to think of the future; I got married in 1973 to Clarena and we had a family on the way. She was an air hostess. The wedding took place in London but we had met while I was on loan to Montreal Olympics in NASL (1971/72) nearly three years earlier. In both my seasons with Montreal I was honored as a second team NASL All Star. I'd been playing for four months, alongside Graeme Souness. Graeme and I became great friends; I enjoyed the experience. So I asked Ron Greenwood for a transfer. Greenwood was having a clear-out at the time anyway, so a lot of first-team players were in the reserves. We were being watched by plenty of scouts.

'I went to Cardiff initially on loan. They were in relegation trouble. I played in the last eight games of the season. In the final match, we were at Ninian Park playing against Crystal Palace. Thirty thousand were there for the game; it was between Palace and us for the drop. We got a draw and stayed up. So I signed for them. That was in March 1974. I played just 100 games, 75 League matches, in three years, scoring five goals. I thought the club was going somewhere. They had good support and a good manager. We went down the next season, though, but we did come back up the next year.

'I'd had a bad injury at Cardiff and had been having a

bit of trouble getting over it. Don Megson, who had been at Bristol Rovers, got the job at Portland and asked me to come over; I really wanted to go to the USA. Everybody was going at the time. It was the best thing I ever did. Clyde [Best] was already playing there, of course. When the time came to leave Cardiff, I was pleased to take Clarena home.'

Clive set up home with Clarena in Portland. They took to Oregon, its climate and people and the apparent appetite for the organised football. Letting it be known he 'could play the piano with his left foot', Clive's ability as a south-paw worked to his advantage, just as it had been the engine that had driven his playing career. Indeed, he was so 'cack-handed', as we say in London's East End, that he once played basketball refusing to leave the left side of the court. But his sense of humour and weakness for practical jokes were the perfect counterpoint to his intelligence and determination. He saw his knowledge of football and wit as the tools he had used to enhance his formative years growing up in London's Docklands. He deployed the same qualities in his coaching career.

'My time with the Portland Timbers was very special. It was the start of all the good things to come for me and my family in America. I was with the Timbers from 1978 to 1981, and played around 70 games. I also played nine games for the Timbers during the 1980-81 NASL indoor season. At the end of the 1981 NASL season I played for Pittsburgh Spirit in the Major Indoor Soccer League and Los

Angeles Lazers. I didn't like that at all but there were bills to be paid. Football gave me the chance to see lots of America, going to away games and changing clubs. You learn about the place and yourself. I got locked out of my hotel room by accident once, in California. I was running round the corridors almost naked, trying hard to look like nothing unusual was happening.

'The Timbers are now a good, good organisation. It was an honour to have been a Timber. If it were not for the Timbers and the support of people like Harry Merlo [a Portland wood manufacturer and philanthropic supporter of sport in Portland] *at that time, the late 1970s, youth soccer in the State of Oregon would not be in the healthy position it is right now. Many of the blokes I played with at Portland are involved with giving chances to our young players. Men like Bill Irwin, Jimmy Conway and Brian Gant have and are making football an attractive and popular game in Oregon. And it all started with the Timbers. I played alongside and against some great players – Jimmy Conway, who was a winger with Manchester City, became the Assistant Coach of the Timbers.'*

I first watched Clive in America at an NASL game at the Robert F Kennedy Memorial Stadium, Washington, DC, and it was clear that he charmed the supporters, many of whom regarded him with the same awe as they might the likes of Pelé, with his hybrid afro/mullet hairdo, his deep-brown eyes and Cockney twang. Like his former West Ham skipper Bobby Moore, Clive always looked immaculate when on the field. His football boots were polished, and his shirt tucked neatly into his shorts. Watching him with the fans after the game, it was clear he had a way of putting them at ease, and he shook my hand when I told him I was from East London and was a West Ham fan. 'You're a long way from home,' he said with mock sternness. 'So are you!' I replied. He laughed and told me I was right. But Oregon was to become as much of a home to him as London's Docklands had been.

As a player, Clive quickly earned a reputation as one of the NASL's best, and hardest, defenders. His quickness on the back line made him an anchor of the Portland defence. He recorded 12 assists and was named three times as an NASL All-Star; he was also selected by Pelé as a member of his all-time greatest NASL team.

After 17 years as a player, Clive embarked on 17 years as a coach. Hundreds of players came from Britain, Europe and South America as part of the NASL invasion of the 1970s; most came to make a relatively easy, comparatively fast buck, but some made a longer-term impact. However, none left a legacy in the USA in quite the same way as Clive Charles. He became a highly respected and trusted coach who touched the lives of those he worked with and among.

He began by driving around the Portland area in an old Volvo, starting up clinics and camps. In 1982, he began his long-term relationship with Reynolds High School that gave rise to the successful Reynolds Lancers team. He was still with the Lazers when Jimmy Conway, a former Timbers team mate, contacted Clive to let him know about a job with Reynold boys soccer team in Troutdale, Oregon. He retired from playing and moved his family back to Oregon. He went on to serve as director of player development for the Oregon Youth Soccer Association. Thus, Clive became a part of Portland, and his work produced the blood for the pumping heart of soccer in the Rose City. He created a strong youth programme that persists to this day, creating, in 1986, F.C. Portland, a local youth soccer club. The club fields numerous youth teams in local, state and national competitions.

But Clive is best known for the University of Portland teams that, after his appointment as soccer director in 1986, claimed a place among the best in the USA for many of the seasons under Clive's guidance.

'After a pretty successful career, I went into coaching and just went from strength to strength, I suppose. The Portland Academy has grown from 20 kids when we started; now we have about 400 families involved.

'When I was playing for West Ham, even at 20 and 21, I was coaching in schools, doing clinics and so on. So it was a long time ago I realised I had something to say, and thought that it was good enough for people to want to listen. I had the ability to teach, but I didn't know much about anything other than football. I probably see myself not so much as a coach but more as a teacher. I'm able to get information over to people in a way that seems to make sense to them and I enjoy sharing that. I am not so much result-oriented as teaching-orientated. If it becomes all about winning, all you get is frustrated when you lose. But I tend to ask questions like, "Why didn't we connect up

with that pass? Why did that work and that didn't?" I can't say results were secondary, but they were kind of linked up with everything else.

'I think you always look to the next game – how are we going to make it better, not perfect, but nearer perfect? I get a lot out of getting players to improve their game but also develop as people. I think the two things can be connected.

'My style seemed to work, but I think that Portland University was ready for soccer. After two years, we organised our tournament and 1,000 people turned up. The previous year there had been about 40. In the first year, it was 8-8-3 then it was 13-7-1, but our schedule was not good. In the third year, we got Kasey Keller and there was a paying crowd of 3,000 to watch us play Santa Clara. It was then I knew we had something.

'By the next week, a little press box had been thrown up and we're thinking we needed to construct a stadium! A couple of years before, we were lucky to get 500 paying nothing! Next thing, a stadium's being built.

'In 1989 I got asked if I would look after our women's programme. I knew nothing about women's football, partly because they were at home when the men were away and I was with the men. But I said I'd do it, but only if the programme was brought up to the same standards that we had with the men. We couldn't get a sniff of the ball when we played UC Santa Barbara and then I knew we'd got a job on our hands.

'In the second year, I signed Tiffeny Milbrett; she was marvellous. She turned the programme round more or less *on her own. It went from something that was just average, and we got a top-ten team. After that, I would say to our players, "You are here because of what Tiffeny did. If she hadn't come to the University, we would not have won a match and you wouldn't have wanted to come here."*

'I don't really have a preference between coaching men and women, probably as I see no difference between what has to be done, although you probably have to approach each of them differently. When women are with women and men are in the company of men, we act differently than, say, when men are with women. That's no secret and it's just how it is. What I would say to any coach, coaching men or women – be as honest as you can with your players.

'I don't think I'd come back to England. In fact, it is probably true that the best thing I ever did was leave England. Living and working in America has made me a better coach. I think, if I'd have stayed in England, I'd probably have been quite restricted in what I could have learned. For every John Lyall, there were a dozen who really didn't have much idea what coaching was about and, in the Seventies, no one in the English game was prepared to learn from other sports or the way things were done in South America or Europe. Look how Malcolm Allison had to struggle at West Ham in the Fifties and Sixties just to try things that had been successful abroad. I know that is changing now, but, even at this time, the English game is a bit inward looking.

'In the United States, you sort of get a bigger picture. If I

155

sat down and chatted to people I played with in England, and talked to them about coaching, they probably wouldn't understand what I was talking about. Harry Redknapp, he's a great guy, but he would have no idea, and he played in the US for a bit. That's not having a go at him; it is just the environment he's in.

'In England, it is getting to be a case of "buy, buy, buy", and, if you get one out of three or four right, that's OK. You can always sell the ones that didn't work, if not for what you paid for them. It's all a bit frantic, almost panicky at times. Players come and go in what seems like no time and there is no time to establish any kind of identity with a club. So you end up with three or four clubs dominating things and then about a dozen or so clubs with nothing to choose between them, as all the players are at about the same level; good enough to be where they are, but not good enough to be playing for the very top clubs.

'Look at the game in England now and almost any team of about 15 could end up in fourth or fifth place in the League by the end of the season. That, up to a point, is good, but there is practically no chance of the same clubs winning the League or even a major trophy. So success is finishing tenth! Then, when the European or World Cup comes along, everyone thinks England are going to win it. But, if you are brought up on the idea that coming tenth is good, how are you in the right frame of mind to actually win?

'Winning is not everything... in fact, it is just something, but the ambition, the want to do as well as you can is

important, and that has to be based on an idea of what real success is. Young fans, young players who turn out for their schools, can take that sort of thing into their everyday lives. Why should anyone be satisfied by second best? Again, there is nothing wrong with coming second, but that shouldn't stop you from trying to be first or even a better second.

'I wouldn't have had the opportunity to coach women in England, certainly not to the highest standard, and coaching women has taught me patience and, as such, made me a better coach. You have to be ready to learn things from your players to be the best possible coach. There comes a point when things are going really well, when you are learning as much from each other and it isn't just one way. I'm not sure many coaches in England have a chance to get to that point. Probably, there are too many demands to produce performances overnight. But you can only teach a player so much; after that, your job as a coach is learning as much as you can about them – how you can put them in a place where they can be the best they can be, and in a position that is most useful to the team? That is about collaboration, working together, and that, of course, takes trust.

'Trust is something given and you are honoured when it is given. But, to get trust, you have to give it. I think that is kind of hard in the game in England right now. That's a shame because, without trust, there can be no respect – so fear and threat take over and eventually that gets destructive. Where I coach, at Portland University, we've

been lucky to have some good people on the staff and some good people playing. Together, we've managed to build something bigger than a football programme. It is a bit like West Ham used to be… there's a family atmosphere and people feel a loyalty to the place and each other. That goes beyond football, really. In the end, that is the biggest thing any sport can do - become the source of something that endures throughout your life.

'I've coached Portland University and American national squads, and being with West Ham has a lot to do with that. I think, if you learn from your experiences in the game, it's all good. Not getting into the side might be seen, over a broader view of things, as being as good for me than, say, if I have gotten a consistent place in the first team. If you want, you can learn as much from the knock-backs as anything else. In fact, I think we learn more from having to do what is hard. That's what I think a coach can do, help players see the wider implications of what is happening to them because of their involvement with the team. That way, football can help you live your life and is not just an end in itself.

'Why does someone support West Ham? It's not because they keep winning, is it? Yes, some people living in East London say they support Liverpool or Manchester United, just because they want to be linked with the success of those teams, but, when Arsenal start dominating, they will just change their shirt from one to the other. That's not really support. No, you support West Ham because they are your team. You are loyal to them. You are committed. That

is a fine quality in a person. So, shouldn't we reinforce loyalty and commitment and ask questions when people are just fickle? Your dad or mum might not be as successful as some mums and dads, your wife might not be the most beautiful woman in the world, but do you leave them because of that? No, we find things in each other. We learn to love what can't be seen and see other types of success. That the Portland players and staff care about the fans who come to watch makes everyone feel part of something and there is reward in success and there is reward in being supportive to each other in failure. We'd better learn to do that in life, because most of us are going to have our fair share of failure; we have to, in order to achieve any kind of true success.

'Unlike some other sports, your place in a soccer squad is reliant on the decisions of others; you can do so much about that, do your best and so on but, at the end of the day, you have to learn to deal the best you can with the cards you are dealt. If you can do that, make the most of whatever it is you're given, then you must be successful.

'At West Ham, John Lyall and Bobby Moore showed me that you can make something out of nothing. How much more can you do with a bit more than nothing? We built a soccer tradition in Portland out of some footballs in the back of an old car! A difficulty young people have today (not just young people, maybe) is that they always seem to need or want more. It seems harder to make the most of any little opportunity. A place in the side is not enough; it has to be a guarantee of a place.

'The reality is, of course, that we mostly just get the one chance and it is up to no one but us to make the most of it. You miss a chance on goal, no one is going to say, "Shame, why don't you have another pop?" The next chance you get it will be up to you to make the best of it. This, I think, is the job of a coach to teach this sort of thing.

'Sport gives opportunities to learn about this stuff in a very real way. We do that in Portland and I know it works. It's not that young people are just "bad" or "spoiled", that's too easy, although some undoubtedly are, but in the main it's because they haven't had the chance to learn the lessons. We all have to learn these things by experience – no one can just be told and then get it. It's like saying, "There aren't enough black managers" and that "Someone should do something about it." Sure, "they" should, but you can't wait for "them" to help you – you might wait for ever! You should do something about it!

'What's the good of being given something just because of the fact that you "are" something – a woman… black? That is just as racist as not being given something because you are black. If you want something, you got to go out and get it; that's a rule of life, no matter what or who you are. You can't expect to be given chances; you got to make the world give you a chance. There's plenty of examples of people doing just that, so it's not just a case of saying it's OK for me to say that.

'In the Under-23 US national side, I've had a midfielder who starts for Ajax; I've had a right-back that plays for Hanover; I had Kasey Keller at Portland. Bruce had coached at Seattle, and it was only because I knew Bruce Rioch when he was at Millwall that Kasey got his chance in England.

'I love Harry Redknapp, but, when I was assistant manager with the US World Cup team, I told him about a good player we had. He said to me, "You've been away a long time. Things have changed." We had just played Brazil and Argentina! People in England still think the US is behind, but Joe-Max Moore scored goals in England and he couldn't even get into the US side. MLS [Major League Soccer] has created a great improvement in young American players, as it puts them in a professional environment; they are better all round than earlier generations.

'But the best thing to come out of my coaching in the US is the FC Portland youth club. I'm proud of that, and the successes of the players that came out of that – Yari Allnutt, for instance. He was a good midfielder for the United States, good enough to go to the 1992 Olympics in Barcelona. He played in the MLS for Kansas City and New England Revolution and Rochester Rhinos in United Soccer Leagues. There was Kasey Keller, who you'd know about, as well as Steve Cherundolo, Conor Casey and, on the women's side, Shannon MacMillan, Tiffeny Milbrett and Michelle French, who played for the US and Washington Freedom. We started the club and I'm the executive director. In 1994, our Under-18s won the USYSA [United States Youth Soccer Association] national title.

Portland is now my home; I love it here. My kids are Americans. My son, Michael, he's a golf pro. My daughter

Sarah studied for her Masters degree at Oregon State University. She played in defence for Portland in the Collegiate First Division [a very good standard] *from 1994 to 1997. Bobby Howe, who was national coach and is now head coach with the Timbers, he's a former Hammer, too, as you'll know.*

Jimmy Gabriel, who played for Scotland, and myself all say that we are better coaches for being in the US. It's a melting pot here. It's more flexible; you have to adapt, be open to new ideas. You pick up things from grid-iron football and basketball. All sport in the US starts in the universities, so we get to work with the cream. After turning out for Portland University, most of the players go on to become pros. I had three girls from my Portland women's side in the US Women's World Cup-winning team. They can earn between $500,000 and $1.5 million a year here. Our women get bigger crowds than lower-division matches and some as good as some of the better clubs in England.

I've been offered more money and the opportunity to coach in MLS. I've had chances to coach at bigger schools and I can't say I wasn't tempted, because it meant a bigger office, prestige, better facilities and a much bigger budget. But I didn't really want to leave. I think it's easier to leave a place that was already established when you went there. But, after building the place yourself, it's tough to leave. It is a good place for me to be and give a little back. I owe a lot to the game, everything really. I will never be able to repay what it's given me, but Portland has been a good place to give what I can.'

162

Clive always remained true to his West Ham roots, as was made obvious when he was asked how the US 2000 Olympic team that he took charge of would play. His answer was short and clear: 'The US is going to play an attacking, entertaining style of soccer.'

The USA were in Group C, along with the Czech Republic (who had just finished second in the European Under-21 finals), Cameroon (an experienced Olympic power that included five players from their World Cup '98 squad, ten of whom had played in the national team that had been victorious in the African Nations' Cup during the winter) and Kuwait, who were a young squad but had experience in the Asian Cup. It was clear to Clive that the Americans' task was neither straightforward nor easy, so he made no predictions about medal prospects but, instead, focused on making the Games an enjoyable experience for his players that would provide a high quality of competition against good opponents. He said, 'I didn't want to repeat the experience of World Cup '98. The "win-no-matter-what" attitude did no good for the team's morale and so their game wasn't as good as it might have been.'

But the USA were resolute in wanting to do better than past teams. Only once, in 1924, had America gone into the final stages of the tournament, and that was only the preliminary round. Seven Olympic competitions went by before the USA got their next win. That was in 1984. After that, there were two more victories, over Kuwait in 1992 and Tunisia in 1996.

The US team was the most experienced ever sent to play

in the Olympics; 13 of the players had MLS experience, and four had played for European clubs. Fifteen had been to the FIFA World Championships at Under-17 or Under-20 level. The squad included three over-age players: defenders Frank Hedjuk, Jeff Agoos and goalkeeper Brad Friedel. These three, together with Ben Olsen and John O'Brien, both midfielders, had substantial experience of international football.

Other members of the squad included defender Chris Albright, who had impressed in the qualifying rounds, Brian Dunseth, Sasha Victorine, the Los Angeles Galaxy striker Josh Wolf, a forward who played for Chicago Fire, and the highly promising Landon Donovan. He was an adaptable striker, who, although just 17 years of age, was thought to represent the future of US soccer. The American strike force looked potent, but the defence seemed, for many, to lack steel. It was perhaps telling that two over-age players were defenders.

The USA started with a 2–2 draw against the Czech Republic. On two occasions, the USA had led the Czechs. Particularly lamentable was the penalty kick conceded after Chad McCarthy had made a late tackle. Conor Casey, Josh Wolff and Chris Albright were unremitting in their efforts against the Czech Republic; Wolff and Albright netted for the USA.

A 1–1 draw followed, this time against the renowned Africans from Cameroon. The match was more one-sided than the game against the Czechs, but again the Yanks could not find that vital final touch. Throughout the whole 90 minutes, John O'Brien was a thorn in the Africans' side, continually identifying and blasting through gaps in

Cameroon's defences. He made an outstanding run, leaving five defenders in his wake, unleashing a dangerous drive in the penalty box that was just off target.

On the cusp of half-time, Wolff scored. But, after Patrick Mboma pulled the Africans level early in the second half, a seemingly legitimate Conor Casey goal was disallowed. However, even the most biased supporter of the 'Indomitable Lions' would admit that the USA were the dominant force in the game and probably deserved more than a draw. For much of the match, the USA threw everything at the Cameroon 'keeper Daniel Bekono, but could not take full advantage of the pressure applied. Bekono produced the performance of his life, one that the Fates usually save for visiting goalkeepers at Upton Park. He denied the USA nine chances, producing remarkable saves, some from point-blank range. Josh Wolff had four clear opportunities that should have been converted into goals in the first half alone and, in the second half, the Americans had a string of chances. But, for all this, a point from the then African Champions, and the eventual gold-medal winners, was a good performance. In fact, as it was clear that Clive's team had bettered their illustrious opponents, the game could be said to have been among the best ever produced by a US soccer team on the international stage.

Nevertheless, Clive subsequently received criticism because he chose not to use the then wonderkid Landon Donovan in an attempt to win the game. Charles explained why he hadn't brought on Donovan, who warmed up for about ten minutes early in the second half. 'I was thinking about using Landon. We were creating opportunities. He is a very good finisher. It was a matter of where we were going to put him. The team was playing very well. The midfield was playing very well and defensively they were closing people down very well. So, if I put Landon in, it would have been up front.

'I needed a big man up there in Conor as a target. As I was thinking about that, Wolfie scored [actually, he set up a penalty kick for Peter Vagenas to score] and two minutes later he made a great near-post run and nearly scored a second one. I thought, you know, I was going to leave things as is.

'Sometimes, you can mess around with things. I just felt that Josh was playing very, very well. I felt we could score another one. I left things alone.'

A little later, Clive was asked why he didn't make even one substitution. His reply was typically to the point and honest: 'You're used to college, son… This is the real game.'

This, of course, did not endear him to a section of the American football press. One particular hack wrote, 'Clive Charles doesn't look like much of a genius these days.'

The response to the result of the Cameroon game might be seen as an example of the insularity of elements within the soccer scene in the USA at the time. The Americans had effectively run all over one of the most dangerous footballing nations in the world, certainly a team worthy of respect as Champions of their continent. That Charles managed to get a point from the game and almost took his side to victory against the mighty Cameroon was deserving of praise rather than derision.

A 3-1 trouncing of Kuwait completed the USA's group commitments. The Kuwaitis never looked like getting much from the game, although it took a Landon Donovan goal two minutes from the final whistle to make the three points secure for the Americans. Many were surprised when Donovan was left out of the first two group games, but against Kuwait he looked phenomenal. Danny Califf opened the scoring with five minutes of the first half remaining and Albright got a second for the USA. This gave Charles and his team the distinction of going into the last eight as group winners.

GROUP C							
	P	W	D	L	F	A	Pts
1.USA	3	1	2	0	6	4	5
2.Cameroon	3	1	2	0	5	4	5
3.Kuwait	3	1	0	2	6	8	3
4.Czech Republic	3	0	2	1	5	6	2

The games against the Czechs and the Cameroonians were held at Bruce Stadium in Canberra and both demonstrated the exemplary standard of American midfield containment. The USA had perturbed the Czech and Cameroon forwards, and laid siege to their defensive ramparts. The effervescent and versatile attack that Clive had crafted had taken command of the opposition by the 25th minute of both games, and it was only a lack of finishing power (a perennial problem for American teams) that stopped the USA from taking full points for their group games.

Japan awaited the USA in the quarter-finals and it was they

who scored first. Wolff then equalised 22 minutes before full-time. But Japan regained the lead just four minutes later. Against the run of play, Vagenas pulled the Americans back into the game with a last-minute penalty. Time not being able to separate the opponents, the tie had to be settled via a penalty shoot-out. The Americans held their collective nerve and took the penalty competition 5–4.

In the end, the game was an even match, but the USA had done well to equal a powerful Japanese team and outgun them when the chips were down. They were now one game from a medal and a possible 180 minutes from Olympic gold. Clive and his boys had surpassed anything done previously by a team from the USA and far exceeded the expectations of most commentators.

America's entry to the Olympic Final was blocked by Spain. The talented Iberians attacked their unsuspecting challengers with a four-man strike force that swiftly penetrated the back line. Early in the game, a quick brace of goals, that were facilitated by mistakes by Danny Califf, more or less killed the match. Spain's front men constantly shuffled and shifted, confusing and confounding the resisting Americans, sophisticatedly breaking through from various angles, consistently out-finessing the US midfield and defence. Vagenas did score another penalty, but the Spanish never really looked in danger of losing a place in the Olympic Final, although the USA did well to hold the score to 2–1 until three minutes from time when Spain gave themselves a two-goal advantage.

It seems the USA must have taken a lot out of the Spanish as they were beaten by Cameroon in the Final. The title had to be settled on penalties after a 2-2 stalemate and the African Champions added the Olympic gold to their list of honours, winning the resultant penalty competition 5-3.

The USA team looked to be relatively demoralised in the bronze-medal match. It seems their spirit had been shaken and this put them at a psychological and physical disadvantage. They were defeated 2-0 by Chile.

This was a disappointing conclusion to a great display by the USA. Clive and his team had good reason to walk away from the Olympics proud of what they had achieved, and that was, by far and away, America's best Olympics soccer tournament ever, and the most notable display by a US men's soccer team in history. It demonstrated the strength of MLS and its ability to produce quality players. By making history for US soccer, Clive had answered his critics in the best possible way, and made a mockery of their damning predictions of humiliation in the competition.

Beyond the tangible accolades involving wins and losses, Clive Charles made a positive and lasting impression on a large majority of players who passed through the soccer programmes at the University of Portland. Clive was a central character in the soccer community in the Pacific north-west of the United States, and the mentor to dozens of American professional players. As a former professional himself, Clive understood the qualities needed to reach and survive at that level. While he was an exceptional coach on the field, he was also gifted in preparing players to make their way in MLS, WUSA (Women's United Soccer Association) or the major European leagues.

For Clive, a crucial factor was being honest in his assessment of a player's ability. He knew that only a truthful appraisal would be authentically helpful in terms of a player making a crucial judgement about their personal future; as good as his Portland teams were, it is still a huge leap from varsity soccer to the cut and thrust of the professional game. And it is not just about being able, it is also a question of timing. For Clive, going to college or playing professionally depended on individual talent but also when that ability can be channelled into a different echelon of the game. So, for Clive, it was true that, if a player was good enough, they should play professionally; but, at the same time, there is a crucial point, a window in time, when that transfer can be most successfully made.

Preparation was critical for Clive. There is a long tradition within Upton Park that goes back to the 1950s. In effect, part of what has become known in the English game as the 'West Ham way' includes an understanding that 'plans go wrong'. A plan is really a belief that people are able to predict the future. It is a bit of a humbling and disconcerting fact to admit that this is just human ego and fantasy. The more elaborate a plan, the more likely it is to fail. In fact, only the most simplistic and short-term plans have much of a chance of working, which begs the question: 'Why bother to make them?'

However, what human beings are good at, what they do almost by instinct, is prepare and adapt to situations. Looking at the way Clive worked, it is obvious that he had embedded this type of attitude into his coaching. He would work all week with the men's or women's teams and allow them to play to their potential in games. Gradually, teams would develop a feeling of fidelity, an understanding which gave rise to an aura of 'readiness'. His 2000 Olympic squad had this characteristic, as did several of the other American teams he took responsibility for; it was a kind of spiritual field effect nurtured through the relationships within squads. It was almost a physical feeling within his programmes at Portland.

However, Clive was more than just a great coach and a capable player. When his name is mentioned to those he worked with and among, they describe him as a genuine, honest person. He was a highly respected man and an inspirational teacher. What Clive's former players remember most about him are the private moments he shared with them, the times when he would chat with them in his office or take a late telephone call from them when they needed advice or just a little comfort.

At Portland, Clive worked with many fine players who would go on to distinguish themselves in the professional ranks, including Scott Benedetti, Nate Jacqua, Ian McLean, Darren Sawatzky, Curtis Spiteri, Davide Xausa, Yari Allnutt and Wade Webber; and with the WUSA, Betsy Barr, Justi Baumgardt, Erin Fahey, Tara Koleski, Erin Misaki, Brooke O'Hanley and Lauren Orlandos. He also worked with Canadian International Christine Sinclair. A few of his highest achievers are listed below to give some idea of the former Hammer's contribution to American and world football.

KASEY KELLER

Born on 29 November 1969 in Olympia, Washington, Kasey started out with Colonial Meats, North Thurston High School, before finding his way to the University of Portland, for whom he played between 1987 and 1990. The 6ft 2in goalkeeper, prior to 2006, appeared four times in the World Cup and was one of the first American goalkeepers to break into the English FA Premier League.

Kasey got his first cap against Colombia on 4 February 1990. After being a member of the US national team in the 1990 World Cup, he was signed by the English club Millwall, becoming a favourite among the South London club's fans during his time there, 1992–96. Keller graduated to the Premiership on signing for newly promoted Leicester City and promptly helped them to League Cup glory in 1997.

After being overlooked by US coach Bora Milutinovic for the 1994 World Cup, Kasey made Steve Sampson's squad in 1998, and played two games in World Cup Finals. Keller was an over-age selection for the 1996 Olympic team, starting all three matches.

Kasey was named US Soccer Athlete of the Year in 1997 and 1999. In 2000, he signed for Spanish club Rayo Vallecano and played there for two years. He returned to England and the Premier League in 2001 with Spurs. At first, he found himself being little more than cover for Neil Sullivan, but he made himself first choice, and was ever-present for Tottenham throughout the 2002/03 and the 2003/04 seasons.

Kasey, second choice to Brad Friedel – Blackburn Rovers' goalkeeper at the time of writing – in the 2002 World Cup, has amassed 100 caps for the USA and is his nation's all-time leader in wins and keeping clean sheets (shut outs).

Playing in the USA's historic 1998 victory against Brazil, Kasey made a number of crucial saves to preserve the Americans' 1–0 lead. His performance prompted the great Brazilian Romario to remark, 'That is the best performance by a goalkeeper I have ever seen…'

In the 2004/05 Premiership season, Kasey fell out of favour at Tottenham as Paul Robinson took the number 1 shirt. In November 2004, Kasey went on a month's loan to Southampton, a Premiership club ravaged by injuries to its goalkeeping personnel, for one month.

On 15 January 2005, Kasey joined Borussia Mönchengladbach on a free transfer during the Bundesliga's winter break. He got off to a good start in Germany, keeping a clean sheet in his first appearance. Kasey held on to the 'keeper's jersey throughout the second half of the season, seven times walking away unbeaten and so playing an important part in saving the club from relegation.

Kasey crowned his nation's run in the 2005 CONCACAF Gold Cup tournament with a clean sheet in the final match against Panama and two saves in the penalty shoot-out gave the USA one of its greatest ever triumphs. Kasey started the first seven games of the final round of World Cup qualifying in 2005, recording 507 scoreless minutes in a run of five clean sheets. This led to the USA qualifying for the 2006 World Cup Finals in Germany. He then became the first male player in US history to win his third Athlete of the Year award. On 2 May 2006, Kasey and team-mate Claudio Reyna became the first two Americans named in four World Cup team sheets.

He played in all three games in Germany, being named Man of the Match in the 1-1 draw with Italy in Kaiserslautern on 17 June 2006.

On 10 August 2006 Kasey was selected by his teammates to captain club side Borussia Mönchengladbach during the 2006-07 campaign, becoming only the second American (Claudio Reyna being the first) to skipper a top level German side.

Almost exactly a year later Keller returned to the English Premier League with Fulham as cover for Antti Niemi, but some poor displays by Niemi saw Kasey take over as first choice keeper at Craven Cottage for a short period of time. However, the day before the Premier League match against Derby County in October, Keller injured his arm in training and looked to be out of the game until early 2008.

KASEY KELLER'S CAREER RECORD

GAMES PLAYED		
1992-96	Millwall FC	176
1992-96	Leicester City FC	99
1996-99	Rayo Vallecano	51
1999-2001	Tottenham Hotspur FC	85
2001-04	Southampton FC	4
2005-2007	Borussia Mönchengladbach	78
2007-	Fulham	3
1988-	United States	102

Kasey said of Clive Charles, 'Clive was more than a mentor; he was the person that I took so much out of. To me, he was family.'

Kasey Keller was one of Clive's first players to go to Europe in 1990, and he believes his choice of Portland as his school changed his life. 'It was the smartest career move I ever made. Clive and [assistant coach] Bill [Irwin] really set me up perfectly to be the first American kid to go over [to England]… I owe a lot to Clive and Bill for preparing me very well to go over and not be surprised by anything that was thrown at me.'

CHRIS BROWN

Chris Brown grew up in Portland, Oregon. His parents introduced him to soccer when he was five years old, and he was coached by his father in the first couple of years of his childhood playing career. By the time he was eight, Chris had begun to be involved in competitive games with FC Portland where he played until he went to college. He led FC Portland to an Under-18 National Championship.

Brown represented the USA at Under-17, Under-18, Under-20, Under-23 and Olympic levels. This being the case, Chris was a strong college prospect. But his ambition since the age of ten had been to work with Clive Charles, his club coach during his time at Jesuit High School. As a freshman at Portland University, Chris's team got to the Final Four.

Chris scored 33 goals in his Portland career, and was named in the All-West Coast Conference First Team in his senior year. After four years at Portland, Chris left to train with the US Under-23 squad and caught the eye of the Kansas City Wizards' head coach, who told Brown he was going to draft him. Chris was selected in the first round (sixth overall) of the 1999 MLS College Draft. With the Wizards, Chris's goalscoring talent put him ahead of all the rookies.

In 2000, Chris Brown was part of the Wizards squad that won the MLS Cup. During the 2003 season, Chris was transferred to New England. He endeared himself to Revolution fans by scoring a hat-trick in his first game at Gillette Stadium during a 5–1 win over the Chicago Fire. That was the first and only hat-trick of Chris's career and the fourth in Revolution's history.

On 8 April 2004, Chris moved to the San José Earthquakes. Although only playing a total of 561 minutes in 11 games for the Earthquakes (seven starts), Chris demonstrated his ability as a dangerous striker, netting twice on 8 May 2004 against Metro Stars and grabbing another on 4 September against New England.

Following the 2004 season, Chris joined Real Salt Lake. He played 29 games for RSL, making 25 starts as a utility player, covering three different positions (forward, midfield and defender). On 16 July, Chris scored his first goal for Real in the tenth minute of a match at Kansas City.

Looking back at his time at Portland, Chris recalled, 'When you go to Portland, Clive is pretty much a father figure to the girls and the boys. He takes you almost as his son or daughter... I knew I'd have my best chance to be a pro with a coach like Clive... He told me that, if I came to Portland, I would leave a better player. If I wanted to be a professional, I would be a professional. And he did just that. Charles doesn't separate his men's and women's teams; they hang out together every night, every day.'

Paradis Ariazand had joined the women's team during Chris Brown's senior season at Portland and they started a relationship; they were married a year later. On 9 July 2007, Paradis gave birth to a baby girl, Baily Brown – a good name for a soccer player. Ariazand played one season for Clive, then joined Chris with Kansas City with her coach's blessing. According to Chris, 'She had a long talk with Clive and he told her to do what she needed to do. I owe a lot to him.'

KELLY GRAY

Kelly Gray was born on 7 April 1981 in Palo Alto, California. He is currently a defender with Los Angeles Galaxy in the MLS.

Kelly played forward and midfielder at the University of Portland from 1999 to 2001. He scored 32 goals in his three years for the Pilots (Portland University's first team) and was voted a second-team All-American and first-team All-WCC (West Coast Conference) as a junior.

In 2001, Kelly played for the US Under-20s in the World Youth Championship in Argentina. By that time, he was beginning to attract interest from European clubs and the MLS. When Kelly talked about his options, he said, 'I'm going to go back home [after the tournament] and talk to Clive... Whatever Clive thinks is best for me, that's what I'm going to do.'

Kelly played one more season at Portland before turning

pro and having a very solid rookie year. Apparently, Clive knew when Kelly was ready to leave.

After his junior season, Kelly signed a Project-40 contract (Nike Project 40 allows younger players to compete at professional levels while still attending college) with MLS, and was selected fifth overall in the 2002 MLS SuperDraft by the Chicago Fire. Kelly made an immediate impact with the Fire, starting 20 games as a rookie while scoring two goals and five assists. He appeared in 28 games in 2003, again starting 20, while scoring two goals and one assist. On 20 January the same year, he captained the American Under-23 team. While playing more defensively in 2004, he started 23 games for the Fire, scoring one goal.

Kelly's versatility has not been entirely advantageous in terms of his development; three years into his career with the Fire, it was still unclear what his position should be. Although a consistent starter, Kelly wanted to return to his hometown and subsequently joined the San José Earthquakes in June 2005. Along with the rest of his Earthquakes team-mates, he moved to Houston for the 2006 season. In June 2007, Kelly moved to Los Angeles Galaxy (Nate Jaqua went to Dynamo as part to the same deal). His debut game for Galaxy, on 4 July 2007, was a 2-0 win over Chicago.

STEVE CHERUNDOLO

A US national team player, Steve is small but swift, with good man-marking ability and passing skills. A defender for both club and country, Cherundolo has become a consistent presence on the right side of the US defence. Steve's goal against Germany on 22 March 2006, from 70 yards, is considered to be one of the longest-range goals in US history.

Steve was the West Coast Conference Freshman of the Year following his first year at the University of Portland in 1997. He left after his sophomore season to begin his professional career in January 1999 with Hanover 96. After helping Hanover gain promotion to Germany's top division in 2003, he became a regular fixture in their line-up at right-back.

Steve travelled to Jamaica to make his US international debut on 8 September 1999. A member of the 2005 CONCACAF Gold Cup-winning side, Steve had trained with the full US men's national team in San Diego prior to the 1998 World Cup and has been a regular in the American national side ever since 1999 (apart from when prevented by injury). He made his debut in the Under-23 side as an 18-year-old against Canada on 28 March 1998. He 'co-captained' the US Under-20 men's national team to an 11th place finish at the 1999 FIFA World Youth Championship in Nigeria, having experience in all four of the US U-18 national team's international matches in 1997.

On 22 March 2006, Cherundolo was a member of the US side that played Germany, a team that included some of his teammates from Hannover 96. Steve scored his first international goal in America's 4-1 defeat. On 2 May 2006, for the second successive time, Cherundolo was named on the US roster for the FIFA World Cup in Germany.

Steve recalled the guidance Clive gave him when Steve was trying to make up his mind about turning professional, saying, 'He told me, "When you're ready, I'll send you on your

179

way. Until then, I need all your efforts."' Clive eventually told him it was time to go following his sophomore season.

Steve also gave an insight into Clive's approach to the game, observing, 'When Clive wins, it's great for him, but I don't think it's on top of his list... Players becoming complete, living up to their abilities... That, I think, makes him most happy.

'He definitely left his mark... Some of the things he tried to instil in his players were to take care of the little things and the big things would take care of themselves. He tried to teach you to be a good person.

'He taught me how to grow up. You get that right, and everything else is easy... Even though he wanted me to become a good player, he was more concerned with me as a person and how I developed into a better man as opposed to a better player... He was just a class act... If people remember him as that and try to continue those ways, then I think he will certainly have left his mark.'

CONOR CASEY

Conor led the US 2000 Olympic men's soccer team to their historic fourth-place finish, having started all of America's half-a-dozen games in Sydney. After returning to the University of Portland, where his 23 goals had led the nation's scoring charts, he had a choice to stay with the Pilots or move on to Germany, having the opportunity to play for Borussia Dortmund as well as fielding offers from a number of other leading clubs. The choice was not a hard one for the boy from Denver.

Conor, who had played for the US Under-18 national team, recalled, 'After one year with Clive, my game just doubled and tripled. It was really amazing how quickly I improved working with him... Clive is the man responsible for preparing me as a player for the professional game. He showed me how to make that step... I benefited from him being a professional.'

On completion of his sophomore year in Oregon, Conor left Portland in 1997 with Clive's blessing.

Casey played at the 2001 World Youth Championship in Argentina and has since graduated to the senior US national team, getting his first of eight caps on 31 March against Poland.

Having played for Dortmund reserves for a year, Conor was loaned out in the 2001–02 season to Steve Cherundolo's second division club Hannover 96, where he scored seven goals in 19 games, helping the club achieve promotion. He remained with Dortmund in 2002–2003 but played just four games, scoring a single goal. In 2003–4, he was once more loaned to a second division club, Karlsruhe, where he established himself amongst the best young forwards outside the top-flight, hitting 14 goals in 30 matches. Before the 2004–05 season, Conor was sold to Mainz for around €300,000.

Early in February 2007, Conor moved to MLS expansion side Toronto FC. However he was traded to the Colorado Rapids in April 2007 in exchange for cash and Riley O'Neill.

He once said of Clive Charles, 'As a person, what was different about him was just pure honesty... He meant everything he did, and he wanted to be that way even if other people did not agree with him. Alongside my parents, he always reminded me that there were more important things to life than soccer.'

TIFFENY CARLEEN MILBRETT

Tiffeny Milbrett was born on 23 October 1972 in Portland and grew up in Hillsboro, Oregon, with her mum and older brother Mark. She was a two-time *Parade Magazine* All-American while attending Hillsboro High School in Portland and holds the Oregon high-goalscoring record, having netted 54 times in her high-school career.

In 1990, Tiffeny enrolled at the University of Portland. That same year, she was named Soccer America's National Freshman of the Year, being her team's top goalscorer with 18 and Portland's MVP (Most Valued Player). The following year, she led the team with 25 goals and six assists.

Tiffeny was then invited to join the Olympic Development Programme. She did so well that a scout invited her to train with the national team when she was 16. She missed her high-school graduation to travel to Bulgaria with the Under-20 national team and was a member of the Under-20 team that won the 1993 International Women's Tournament in Montricoux, France. She was also in the US team that won the silver medal at the 1993 World University Games in Buffalo, NY.

In 1994, Tiffeny topped the American charts with 30 goals and eight assists. She was tied with Mia Hamm as the National Collegiate Athletic Association's leading goalscorer in Division I colleges.

Tiffeny is a three-time participant of the US Olympic Festival, playing for the West in 1990, 1993 and 1994, winning a gold medal in 1993, a silver in 1994 and she was a three-time (1991, 1992 and 1994) NSCAA (National Soccer Coaches Association of America) All-American. She was also West Coast Conference Offensive Player of the Year in 1992 and 1994.

Tiffeny was part of the US team that won the title at the 1994 CONCACAF Qualifying Championship in Montreal and she helped the team to qualify for the 1995 FIFA Women's World Championship in Sweden where America finished third. Tiffeny, then 22, was summoned off the bench to replace Michelle Akers, the first superstar of women's football. Tiffeny scored, finishing that tournament with three goals to her credit, equalling Kristine Lilly and Tisha Venturini for top goalscorer for her team in that tournament.

Tiffeny was a member of the gold medal-winning US women's national team at the 1996 Centennial Olympics. She scored two goals during the Games, including the match-winner against China to capture the gold medal.

In 1995 and 1996, Tiffeny turned out for Shiroki Serena in the women's J-League in Japan.

Tiffeny was top US goalscorer during the historic 1999 FIFA Women's World Cup. In the 2000 Olympic Games in Australia, she helped to lead her team to the silver medal. She scored twice in the gold-medal game, including a dramatic equaliser in stoppage time. In the 2000 CONCACAF Women's Gold Cup, Tiffeny scored seven goals and was named MVP.

In 2001, Milbrett finished a controversial third in voting

behind US team-mate Mia Hamm and Chinese superstar Sun Wen for the FIFA Women's World Player of the Year.

Tiffeny went on to play for the WUSA with eight teams, the last of which was New York Power.

Tiffeny, whose blunt remarks have earned her the nickname 'No Tact Tiff' from her team-mates, was, as a player, able to combine sizzling speed with outstanding technical ability. A diminutive but explosive striker, she was recognised as one of the world's best when running with the ball at her feet and creating dangerous scoring opportunities.

WUSA Commissioner and former US coach Tony DiCicco said of Tiffeny, 'I remember watching highlights of how Ronaldo would make world-class defenders look like they were running in sand... Tiffeny has that same quality. When she puts it into gear, she just freezes people. She has to be the most exciting player to watch in the world...'

Following differences with coach April Heinrichs, Tiffeny's international career appeared to be over. In March 2005, she went to Sweden for two months, scoring five goals for Sunnanå SK. When Heinrichs resigned in February 2005 and was replaced by Greg Ryan, Tiffeny returned to the Americas, Vancouver Whitecaps Women and the US national team to. She gained her 200th cap on 30 June in a friendly v Canada. Her 100th goal came in Team USA's next match, a friendly against Ukraine in her hometown of Portland.

The all-time leading scorer in WUSA history, Tiffeny almost single-handedly carried the New York Power to the playoff semi-finals in the first season of the WUSA and was named MVP and Offensive Player of the Year. She scored more goals than all the rest of her team-mates put together, which is an unprecedented achievement at the game's highest level.

When asked who had been the most influential person in her life, Tiffeny named Clive Charles. When questioned about which coach was most influential in her career, again she named Clive Charles. It was the same response when she was called upon to name who she saw as the best coach in the world.

Tiffeny grew up watching the Portland Timbers and attending the team's summer camps. Clive, a defender by instinct and practice, was among the players who worked with her. She joined his FC Portland women's team when she was 15 and, as such, going to Portland University was something of a natural course of action for the young striker. She joined the Pilots in Clive's second year as women's coach. According to Tiffeny, 'I never would have thought to go anywhere else… and I wouldn't have gone there if not for him. I didn't go for the school, I didn't go for the education, I went because Clive asked me to. When he asked, I said yes within a half-second, without any thought.'

Clive became the male role model in Tiffeny's life. She said, 'I didn't have a father in my life. He filled that void… I don't know if he'd like me saying that, but it's true. When you talk about guidance, support, trust and love, those are things you get from your parents.' For Tiffeny, Clive provided 'everything you'd want from a family, to feel respected and understood and trusted… There's a real, real close bond, very tight-knit, very special. If you didn't go to Portland, you'd never understand it.'

According to Tiffeny, Portland soccer means as much to her

now as it did when she was at the University. In fact, on reflection, 'It might be more important to me now. I understand things more. I have a better perspective. My blood's purple [Portland's colours]. I think everyone else would say that, too.'

SHANNON ANN MACMILLAN

Shannon is able to play in midfield or attack. A skilful dribbler, Shannon also has one of the hardest shots in the women's game; she is tremendously strong and fast and able to wear down defenders.

Shannon was the youngest member of the US women's national team that won the silver medal at the 1993 World University Games in Buffalo, NY, where she made her debut as an international player. In that same year, she was part of the US women's Under-20 national team that won an International Women's Tournament in Montricoux, France.

Shannon, who was named as the Soccer America Player of the Year in 1995, was originally left off the roster for the residential training camp leading up to the 1996 Olympics. But, having been brought into the squad at a relatively late stage, she scored the winning goals in both the semi-final (against Norway) and gold-medal game (against Sweden) to help the USA to victory. Shannon walked away from the Games as her nation's top scorer with three goals in five matches. Her 'golden goal' against Norway was one of the most important in US soccer history, putting America into the Olympic Final and avenging the loss at the 1995 FIFA Women's World Cup.

Shannon was a member of the USA's gold-medal team at the 1998 Goodwill Games and the following year at the Women's World Cup. She played in all six matches, but started just one, against North Korea. However, her influential part in the match was noted and she recorded one of the biggest assists in US history, providing the corner-kick for Joy Fawcett to head home the winning goal in the quarter-final against Germany just seconds after taking the pitch. She took the field in the 57th minute of the Final against China, replacing Cindy Parlow, so proving herself more than worthy of her winner's medal.

Shannon played in 26 games for the USA in 1999, scoring eight goals with 14 assists and became just the 12th player in US history with 20 or more career goals. In 2000, Shannon was one of the US team to claim Olympic silver.

At club level, Shannon played for the La Jolla Nomads, who won the State Club Championship over two consecutive years (1991 and 1992), winning the Western Regionals in 1991, before going on to finish second at the National Championships. In the 1996 and 1997 seasons, Shannon appeared in the Japanese women's professional league with Shiroki Serena alongside college and national team-mate Tiffeny Milbrett.

As assistant women's soccer coach at Portland, in her first year in the role, Shannon helped the team make the 1998 NCAA (National Collegiate Athletic Association) Final Four. But she continued to be an active player, and was elected to the All-WUSA First Team in 2001 and was San Diego Spirit's MVP. She was also named as the 2002 Chevy Female Player of the Year. On 26 April 2003, she scored four goals in the USA's win over Canada.

Shannon earned a place on the roster for the 2003 Women's World Cup team. She was one of the founding players of the Women's United Soccer Association's San Diego Spirit.

MacMillan retired from international football in 2006 at the age of 31 with 60 goals and with 175 caps; only nine woman in history had played more times for the US. She was inducted into the Oregon Sports Hall of Fame on 25 September 2007.

When asked about the effect Clive Charles had on her career, Shannon, who left an abusive, shattered home life as 'a shy, quiet, timid individual' to join Charles at Portland, said, 'I definitely owe my career and where I am today to that man... He basically turned my life around. When I took that Greyhound bus [from San Diego] to Portland, I got off a weak, timid, unconfident little girl who didn't know her potential or how to achieve it. Really, through his teaching, friendship and love, he became the father figure I'd never had... I didn't really have a lot of confidence when I came to Portland, and he helped me become a happy, confident person... Hands down, I owe everything I have achieved in soccer and where I am with the national team to him.'

Shannon had never met Charles until her recruiting trip to Portland. Before introducing himself, Charles watched how Shannon interacted with the players and coaching staff. He concluded that she would be a good fit into the team and at the school.

Shannon quickly found out that Charles cared about her as

a person. She arrived at Portland in 1992 to find her troubles immediately exacerbated when, during her first week at college, she learned that her best friend from high school had died of heat stroke. She recalled, 'I remember being blown away and wanting to give up and not knowing what to do.'

Clive took her aside and asked, 'Do I think you should be on the field? Yes. But, at the same time, it has to be your decision. If you decide never to touch a ball for me, I will still honour your scholarship. We are here for you.'

'I was just blown away by that,' Shannon recollected almost a decade later. 'This guy actually cared about me as a person first… I literally bit my tongue from saying, "Where do I sign?"'

'He saw something in me that I never knew was there. He helped me believe in myself and gave me tools to achieve every dream I set. There is this utter sincerity about him and he truly cares more about his players off the field than he does on the field.'

Shannon went to Clive with her troubles, 'always bawling my head off'. He kept a box of tissues in his desk, he told her, just for her. She asserted, 'He's truly an incredible and special man… I am where I am as a person and a player because of Clive. I love him. I owe every step of my career and who I am as a person to that man.'

As an assistant coach of the women's team at Portland, Shannon got to see Charles from another perspective. 'He just had a profound knowledge of the game… Just to see the way he handled the men's team differently than he did the women's team. He knew how to deal with women. He could go after the men, and that was going to motivate them.

'Game day, he sat back and became a fan. He did his work all week, and, when game day came, it was our turn to shine and be the individuals we are. You didn't hear him yell during a game.

'Just being in there and seeing how much time and effort he put into preparing for a session and how he worried about people if they were not doing well in school or if they had personal issues; how genuinely he cared about people. He was such a great guy. He could make anyone comfortable and feel like they could conquer the world.

'When I was on the coaching staff, every morning he would ask for an update on someone; how she is doing. He really has his finger on the pulse of all the teams and every individual... I think he has done great in the way he empowers people to empower themselves... People that maybe if they went to another school might not be in the league [WUSA]. Because they went to Portland, they became a great soccer player with a great brain under Clive Charles. That's how they are able to go out in this league and survive.'

WYNNE MCINTOSH
Born 17 October 1975 in Billings, Montana, Wynne helped the Pilots to four straight NCAA Tournaments from 1994 to 1997, including three consecutive semi-final appearances and a trip to the 1995 Championship game. That same year, she was ranked eighth nationally with six game-winning goals. She finished her career as Portland's third all-time leading scorer with 42 goals.

Wynne first met Clive at the age 13 at a soccer academy in

Seattle. 'I distinctly remember some of those sessions... You meet him, and he demands respect. He has a really great way of dealing with players.'

A member of the Under-20 national team pool from 1993 to 1995, Wynne had represented her country at Under-16, Under-17 and Under-18 levels. She also made the West Regional Under-16 and Under-19 teams.

Wynne spent the 1998 season playing professionally in Germany, but was back in America in the role of player-coach for the W-League Denver Diamonds in 1999 and 2000. Wynne spent the 2001 season with California Storm of the WPSL (Women's Premier Soccer League) before signing for New York Power as a free agent in March 2002 and promptly earned a place as a defender. She moved to San Diego Spirit in September of 2002. Wynne played the 2003 season with the W-League Seattle Sounders.

McIntosh, who has the United States Soccer Federation 'B' coaching licence, served as an assistant coach at San José State University in 2001, helping the Spartans to their first WAC Championship and first NCAA playoff berth. She moved on to coach for the Colorado Rush Soccer Club, as well as Emerald City FC in Seattle.

Hired as an assistant coach in June 2002 by Portland University, Wynne entered her fourth season on the combined staff, sharing recruiting and player development responsibilities. Pilot teams have never missed an NCAA tournament throughout Wynne's coaching tenure. She currently resides in Portland with her family.

One of Clive's assistants in 2002, McIntosh recalled, 'I

always felt so bad we didn't win [the Championship] for the school and for Clive… I am so blessed to have him in my life.'

Wynne, who lost her father when she was 13, said, 'I would definitely say that Clive plays a fatherly role. I'm not around him that often, but his presence in my life is definitely as a father figure. I feel like I can go talk to him about anything… Clive simplifies everything. He is just a really, really good teacher. He has such a wealth of knowledge.'

Wynne said that some of her closest friends in college were members of the men's soccer team. 'The guys were playing Central Florida, and all the girls were out there screaming and stuff. Clive kind of encourages that.'

Her abiding memory of her coach is very much akin to most of the other players who were influenced by him. 'He cares about all of us as people… He cares about what's going on in your life, about how your mom's doing, about how your dog is doing.'

JUSTI BAUMGARDT-YAMADA

A left-footed midfielder, clever play-maker, a fine long passer and highly skilled in possession, Justi started her soccer career at a young age. In 1992, she was named Parade High School All-American Player of the Year and the nation's number-one high-school recruit. She was selected as National Player of the Year in 1993 and, in the same year, she was named *Seattle Times* Athlete of the Year, and the House of Representatives in the State of Washington passed a resolution in her name, honouring her election as the Player of the Year and leading Federal Way to two State Championships.

Justi was Portland's MVP as a sophomore in 1995. She scored five goals and registered 12 assists as a sophomore to help the University of Portland advance to the Final Four in Chapel Hill, NC. She scored a goal 12 seconds into a match against San Diego State, the fastest goal in WCC history. Justi started all 21 games for Portland in her freshman season. Her seven goals and 12 assists placed her among the University's top players and helped her earn WCC Freshman of the Year honours.

Elected WCC Player of the Year in 1996, Justi led the league as a goal scorer. That same year, she was ranked fifth nationally with eight game-winning goals and was the Pilots' MVP.

Justi is a three-year NSCAA All-American and two-time NCAA Final Four All-Tournament Team member. In 1997, she scored 11 goals and provided 13 assists to help the Pilots to the West Coast Conference title. She finished her college career as the Pilots' fourth-highest goalscorer with 37 and first in assists with 50. Justi started 84 of 85 games in her college career.

Making her debut with the US women's national team against Canada on 12 June 1993 as an 18-year-old, Justi did not appear as a full international again until 28 February 1997, against Australia in Melbourne. Her debut international goal was the first of the game against Australia in Bathurst on 3 March 1997.

However, between Justi's first and second appearances in the senior team, she was a member of the Under-20 national team and competed at the Nordic Cup in Denmark in August

1993, and again in Germany in August 1994. In April 1993, she was a member of the squad that won the international tournament in Montricoux, France, and participated in the 1997 Nike Victory Tour and US Cup and travelled with the team to Australia, China and Portugal in 1998.

Justi played for New York Power and was with the Sacramento Storm in 2000, but was drafted in 2001 by the Washington Freedom. Now, she's a midfielder with the semi-pro Sounders Saints, playing in the W-League, and splits her parental duties, for her son Caden, with her husband Tote Yamada. She is also Washington Premier FC's Under-18 girls coach and director.

Although Clive worked with both the men's and the women's teams at Portland, as well as giving a huge commitment to the various national sides, according to Justi, 'It was never a problem… He may have missed one or two games at the absolute most.' Recalling her relationship with Clive, Justi said, 'After I graduated and I was training with the national team, I would go back to Portland and train with the men's team. He coaches differently. It's amazing to be able to see the differences.'

She had known Clive since she was 13 years old and wanted to play for him at Portland. 'As soon as I had been coached by him for a few sessions, I knew he was an amazing coach… He knows the game; he understands the game. And the way he can teach the game, he's so good at understanding the different personalities of players. I have spoken to players that have been around Clive that are from other schools, and I've never met anyone that doesn't love the man.'

When former Pilots are asked about their experience of working with Clive Charles, they consistently refer to the intense learning environment he fostered; it was focused, pragmatic and challenging but, for all this, great fun. However, it seems, beyond all the coaching and teaching skills, the root of Clive's impact on the people he worked with was his kindness. Indeed, those who knew Clive best consistently state that there wasn't anyone who had a negative word to say about him. Joe Etzel, Portland's long-serving athletics director, who claimed Clive was the 'best hire' he had ever made, once said, 'Clive was a person you never heard somebody bad-mouth… All the success he had, he didn't seem to have people who were jealous of what he'd accomplished. He was just a great individual.'

Portland senior Imani Dorsey was a member of the 2002 Women's College Cup National Championship team as well as the 2000 and 2001 NCAA Division I National Champion-ship semi-final teams. She was also four-time All-Conference Selection and 2003 Conference Defender of the Year. Imani was Buzz Freshman of the Year 2000 and team captain in 2003. In terms of her achievements, she could be seen as personifying Clive's ability as a coach, but the other side of Clive seemed to be the seed of Dorsey's motivation. She recalled, 'When I first met him, I knew I wanted to play for him… He just commanded your attention and your respect every time he spoke to you. He was pretty much a father figure to almost all of his players.' Imani's reaction and development are indicative of the response of many who worked with and alongside Clive.

Clive originally started the process of creating Portland University's internationally recognised soccer programme in 1986. When he took up the post, he was part of a fairly anonymous athletics department that had very little soccer tradition – indeed, the Catholic University's small enrolment of 2,800 was hard-pressed to discover any real athletes of significant potential in any sporting disciplines, never mind one that had been imported in the previous couple of decades.

He was the third head soccer coach for men in the history of the University. However, at the end of the 1987 season, Portland were third in the WCC. A 3–1 victory over Notre Dame was among the team's 13 wins.

The following year, Clive's men were ranked as high as number two nationally and challenged for the NCAA title, winning their first 21 games. In the Final Four, they were defeated by the eventual Champions, Indiana, but Portland had begun the development of dozens of athletes who would play professionally for various national teams. The playoff appearance was the University's first in soccer. Portland won the first of three straight WCC Championships and four in a six-year period.

In 1989, Clive was appointed as Portland University's director of soccer, and took over as head women's coach, leading the Pilots to a very successful season. The men's team again climbed to number two in the polls and earned the second of six consecutive NCAA berths, reaching the second round. The team finished with the second-best record in school history.

By 1990, Portland's Harry A Merlo Field was one of the nation's best soccer facilities. Clive's men won the WCC title, but lost in the first round of the NCAA playoffs.

The Pilot women won the first of two straight North-West Collegiate Soccer Conference Championships and appeared in the national top 20 for the first time, reaching number 12. Tiffeny Milbrett was named the NCSC (Northwest Collegiate Soccer Coference) Player of the Year and the Soccer America Freshman of the Year. The following season, Tiffeny achieved All-America honours and her second NCSC Player of the Year award while establishing a school record with 25 goals.

The three-year supremacy of the Conference Crown by the Portland men came to an end in 1991, but they reached the post-season's second round. The women also finished the season strongly.

In 1992, Charles led two teams to the NCAA playoffs in the same year, an achievement with little precedent. His women made history, winning a school-record 18 games and earning the University's first women's NCAA playoff berth and the first of seven successive post-season bids. Portland's men achieved number-one national ranking, while the women reached number three in the USA, with Tiffeny Milbrett scoring 30 goals and providing 12 assists. The women joined the WCC and both programmes claimed League Championships. The then biggest crowd in the history of US women's soccer, 5,596, crammed into Merlo Field for the first-ever meeting between Portland and North Carolina, recognised as one of the best teams in the country.

Portland's next campaign, with Clive named as head coach

of the US Under-20 women's team (a post he would hold for three years), saw both the women and men simultaneously earn NCAA playoff berths for the second year in succession. Shannon MacMillan and freshman sensation Justi Baumgardt-Yamada led the Pilots to their first-ever NCAA Playoff win, a 2–0 first-round defeat of Conference rival Santa Clara. Portland lost in the quarter-finals at Stanford by the only goal of the game.

The men concluded their schedule by losing to St Louis on penalty kicks.

The Pilot women recaptured the WCC title in 1994 and reached the NCAA Final Four, staged at Merlo Field. The highly successful but injury-plagued season came to a conclusion with a 1–0 defeat to Notre Dame. The Pilots also placed a record five players on the All-WCC first team.

The run of six consecutive playoff berths achieved by the Pilot men ended, but the team boasted the programme's eighth winning season under Clive's nine years at the helm.

Clive provided commentary and expert analysis for ESPN's (Entertainment and Sports Programming Network) coverage of the 1994 World Cup and received high ratings.

On consecutive weekends in 1995, Clive took both the men's and the women's programmes to their respective Final Fours, making him only the second collegiate soccer coach in history to lead two teams to the NCAA semi-finals in the same year (UNC's Anson Dorrance was the first in 1987). The men's team were defeated in the semi-finals by the only goal of the game. Wisconsin, the team that would be NCAA Champions, became their nemesis at Richmond, Virginia, but

Clive's boys collected 16 wins for the third-best win total in school history.

The women's side lost 1–0 in extra-time to Notre Dame in the National Championship game at Chapel Hill, NC, finishing the year with a school-record 20 wins.

Charles was then named assistant coach of the US men's national team.

The Portland men produced eight wins in their last 11 games of 1996, but failed to gain an NCAA playoff berth for just the second time in nine years. The Pilots' average home attendance of 2,554 was the best in the country.

The Pilot women reached their third consecutive NCAA Final Four, but lost 3–2 to Notre Dame in the semi-finals. Portland finished the season with 19 wins and a third consecutive WCC title. The 1996 Pilot women posted a 21-game unbeaten streak, including an undefeated Conference run, before falling to Notre Dame.

Justi Baumgardt-Yamada became the fifth consecutive Pilot to be named the WCC Player of the Year after Portland's second undefeated Conference season, and the following season she earned her fourth All-WCC first-team honour, becoming just the fourth female WCC player to achieve this. She led the Pilots to a fourth straight WCC title and sixth consecutive NCAA appearance, but a first-round loss at home to UCLA ended a very successful season. With crowds averaging 1,834, the Pilot women attracted the second-highest home attendance in the country.

Early in the season, with the Portland men and women winning on the same day, head coach Clive Charles enjoyed his 300th career collegiate win, making him just the 11th coach in NCAA history to amass that many wins.

The Pilot men lost four of their last six games and missed the NCAA tournament for the second year running; it was the first time since 1988 that the programme failed to take part in post-season play in back-to-back seasons.

The Pilot men finished the 1998 season with two victories but failed to achieve a NCAA playoff berth. Despite a roster decimated by injuries, the Pilot women advanced to their fourth NCAA semi-final in five years, but lost 1–0 to number-one-ranked North Carolina in what would be the longest game in playoff history. Portland's record that season was played 24, won 19, drew three and lost two.

In 1999, the Pilot men, led by all-American freshman forward Conor Casey, ended a three-year playoff drought. Although Portland were at home to Washington, they lost 3–2. However, Conor was the nation's top scorer. Six Pilots were named to the All-WCC team, headed by co-Player of the Year and Freshman of the Year Conor Casey.

The Pilot women concluded their season with a 12-win tally, but still tied for second in the WCC. Portland missed out on its first NCAA tournament in eight seasons. Seven players earned All-WCC honours.

The following season, Clive's women advanced to their fifth NCAA semi-final in seven years, only to lose 1–0 to UCLA. Portland that season won 18 and drew four of their 22 games, winning the WCC title.

Clive directed the men to a number-three ranking, but they missed the playoffs after losing six of the final eight games.

Portland won four of its final five regular-season games to get back into the NCAA playoffs, but again the final glory eluded them. Nate Jaqua and Kelly Gray were named All-Americans. Portland rambled through the NCAA playoffs, winning their first four games by a 15–1 margin, before falling 2–1 to North Carolina in the semi-finals. The Pilots equalled a school record with 20 wins and four draws for the season, and tied for second in the WCC Championship. Freshman scoring sensation Christine Sinclair was named national Freshman of the Year, and was joined on several All-America teams by junior defender Lauren Orlandos.

In 2002, the Pilots claimed their first WCC title since 1992. Portland went on to beat NCAA first-round opponent Oregon State 2–0 before falling to Stanford for the second year in a row; the shoot-out score was 10–9. Nate Jaqua was named an All-American for the second consecutive year. Curtis Spiteri was also named an All-American, while Alejandro Salazar earned WCC Freshman of the Year honours.

The Pilots made history recording the school's first-ever National Championship by defeating Santa Clara 2–1 in double overtime in the College Cup Final. Portland tied the school record with 20 wins for the second consecutive season. Sophomore striker Christine Sinclair confirmed that she was one of the premier collegiate soccer athletes, leading the nation with 26 goals. She was named the WCC Player of the Year, won the Honda Award for best woman collegiate soccer player, and was joined on various All-America teams by senior defender Lauren Orlandos. Freshman midfielder Lindsey Huie was selected the

WCC Freshman of the Year and a first-team freshman All-American.

Over his career as coach of the men's and women's teams, Clive amassed a staggering 439 wins, 144 draws and 44 losses, which included 13 Conference titles (losing only 25 league games), 20 NCAA tournament berths, taking in nine College Cup appearances and seven Final Four appearances. He was one of just five men in NCAA coaching history to win more than 400 college soccer games.

Clive put in 17 seasons as coach of Portland's men's team and 14 seasons with its women's team, and 23 Pilots earned All-America status during Charles's tenure.

The women's programme has claimed seven consecutive post-season berths, advancing to the Final Four in 1994, 1995, 1996 and 1998. The men's team made eight NCAA appearances in the last 12 years of Clive's reign, advancing to the semi-finals in 1988 and 1995.

Clive ranks fifth of all time and was fifth among active NCAA Division I women's soccer coaches in all-time winning percentage – 79.2 per cent.

Clive also spent eight years as a US Soccer staff coach. Late in 1995, Steve Sampson, his former West Coast Conference coaching rival with Santa Clara, named him his top assistant to the men's national team. The USSF had budgeted for a full-time assistant coach and Charles could have stepped down from his post at Portland University, but his loyalty to his players, and the programme he had built, kept him from resigning and, instead, he moonlighted with the national team.

It wasn't the only time Charles turned down an offer to move away from Portland. He could have succeeded Tony DiCicco as coach of the women's national team in 1999 and the University of Connecticut approached him to replace Joe Morrone in 1996. Several MLS teams also courted him, to no avail.

Clive successfully guided the Americans through the qualification games to the 1998 World Cup Finals in France.

In 1997, Clive had been named as coach of the US Under-23 men's Olympic team for the 2000 Olympics in Australia by Sampson. In his first year in the job, his record included two victories over Germany, a 1–0 triumph over Argentina, and a come-from-behind win over Chile.

In Sydney, Clive's tactics and player selections were often questioned by media and fans – not to mention a rather tasteless public display by the father of one of the team's younger players – but in the end it was Charles who had the last laugh as the United States shocked both soccer fans and soccer observers throughout the world by reaching the semi-finals, a best-ever performance for the USA, before falling to a powerful Spanish side.

Clive led a young squad to a third-place finish at the 1997 World University Games in Italy and, in 1999, his Under-23 players achieved third place at the FIFA Confederations Cup in Mexico. In the same year, the team won a bronze medal at the Pan-American Games in Winnipeg, Canada. At the time, Charles commented, 'We're in great shape… US soccer has never been in as good shape as it is right now.'

For all the accolades, the awards and the respect he had

from players, colleagues and fans, nothing can prepare you for the sort of news that Clive heard on 11 August 2000. Clive found out that he had prostate cancer just before departing for the Sydney Olympic Games with the US Under-23 team. He went home that day and told his family and together they experienced the kind of numbness familiar to those who have lived through the shock and fear that accompanies such discoveries. But, for Clive, Australia provided him, as he said, 'with another focus', and this helped.

Clive talked with Tom King, the US national team general manager, and Dan Flynn, the US Soccer Secretary General, and told them he had been diagnosed with cancer. The three agreed to take a week or so to review the situation, but King and Flynn said that Clive was the best person to judge his condition. According to Clive, he felt sufficiently well to continue his role with the American team; his only concern at that point was not wanting to go to the Olympics and attracting attention to his cancer because 'whatever press we were going to get, I wanted it to be about soccer. I didn't want my illness to get in the way of that.' This attitude was typical Clive – he put others ahead of himself, acting as the consummate professional.

Probably the worst time for Clive was when he came back from the Olympics; in the doctor's office after the results of the CT scan had come through, he learned that the cancer had gone from the soft tissue to the bones.

However, hormone therapy had an impact. The cancer stopped growing in the bones for a year. Clive told how he understood the gravity of his situation at the 2001 women's

Final Four. He started to lose his appetite and experience back and hip pain. He was sleeping a lot and the pain was intensified. It was clear that the hormone therapy wasn't working. He recalled, 'Deep down, I knew I was in a battle.'

By January 2002, it was clear the cancer was back in Clive's bones. Radiation therapy followed and Clive suffered some intense pain. The treatment dealt with hot spots – his right shoulder and left hip – but it wasn't killing the cancer. It was just helping with the pain.

He struggled to get out of bed at points. There were prolonged bouts of vomiting and Clive was spending 20 hours a day in bed; he simply couldn't get out. Clarena tried to get him to eat biscuits, but he just couldn't eat or drink. But Clive made himself get up. Some days, he'd just get up, walk around the living room, and go back to bed.

For some time, Clive didn't talk to anybody outside his family; he couldn't take any phone calls. He spent time only with his family. But he received hundreds of cards and emails and they helped a lot. He got cards from all over the world, from people he didn't even know.

Subsequently, in the spring of 2002, Clive was given chemo and, within a week, he was feeling better. Although he was vomiting every day, CT scans indicated that the cancer was shrinking in the bones. It was like a light at the end of the tunnel. He started to get up, walk around the garden, walk up and down the street, walk in the park. He told of how he 'hadn't laughed for so long. And then in June something happened and I had a big belly laugh. I can't remember what it was, but I laughed. I knew I was on my way back.' However, Clive was quite aware that there was no cure for his condition.

A private man, Charles did not publicly disclose his illness until March 2002. By this time, the chemo had seemingly given him a new lease on life, and he was strong enough to coach both Portland teams. However, reflecting on his first day back at work, Clive admitted to being a little scared meeting people again. 'They didn't know what to say; I didn't know what to say.' He started to go in once a week, then twice a week. The first day he spent all day at school was the next big event. 'I actually went in and did a day's work,' he recalled with some amusement.

Pre-season training arrived and Clive didn't know what he would be able to do. He sat and watched training the first day but, within a week, he was coaching, and he coached every day thereafter. But every week, while still coaching, Clive was undergoing the chemotherapy. He described his treatment by saying, 'You just sit there with a drip 'til you're done. I sit there a couple hours, and sometimes I'm sick, and sometimes I'm not. With radiation, I was sick every single day.'

It seemed that six months into the treatment, all reports on Clive were positive.

At the end of what was to be his last season, Clive said he had enjoyed the campaign that took Portland to the NCAA Championship. He said that it had been emotionally no different to any other year, aside from the fact that he'd been tired. The treatments had been rough but, apart from that, he said things had been fine. He had coached both the men's and women's teams at Portland. He had achieved something that he hadn't thought possible and, overall, he had been able to do pretty much what he would have normally done.

In the late summer of 2002, Clive confessed that part of him would have liked to have taken on another role with the US national team, given the joy his work at that level had brought him, and that, if his health allowed him, it was a possibility. However, he admitted that another part of him said to 'keep taking the treatment, wake up in the morning, and keep smelling the roses'.

At that point, he had felt his treatment had gone well, although some days he felt better than others. Seemingly calling on his coaching acumen, Clive saw knowing what to do, learning how to live with that and knowing when to take breaks as important. He said that he had a good staff team, and that they had done a good job of making him stay away sometimes when that was the best thing to do. Clive reflected on how his illness had raised his consciousness of 'a real deep love of family'. He said that 'more than anything, I thought I loved my family, but my goodness!'

Prior to Clive's announcement about his condition, his assistant coaches called several alumni, and urged them to return to Portland. Wynne McIntosh remembered, 'We were in pre-season in Virginia… Garrett [Smith – then assistant coach at Portland] called and said that we should come back to Portland if we could. So we knew something was going on.'

At the time, Wynne was a non-roster player battling for a spot in the New York Power first team. But she felt compelled to make the cross-country trip to be by Clive's side in his time of need.

Wynne and Tiffeny Milbrett flew from Virginia to Portland. They met up with Smith, Shannon MacMillan, and former Portland player Cindy Griffith. Wynne recalled, 'Garrett told us… Clive didn't know we had flown back and we hadn't seen him yet. He walked in and we were all sobbing our brains out. I haven't cried that hard in a long time. His wife Clarena has been unbelievable.' She added that Clive said he had felt the best he had felt in nine years. Wynne, who was in closest proximity to Clive through her role as assistant coach at the University, told how Clive looked well, although he tended to get tired more easily than usual.

Justi Baumgardt-Yamada said at that time, 'The way Garrett says it, is he will eventually die of cancer… But all of us have gotten to tell him exactly how we feel about him. I think it's good that he knows that. We just want to be really encouraging.'

American stars Kasey Keller, Tiffeny Milbrett and Shannon MacMillan were some of Clive's earliest successes at Portland. The seeds he planted in his final classes grow with vigour; players like Canadian international Christine Sinclair and young MLS players like Nate Jaqua and Kelly Gray show his memory won't soon be forgotten.

When the players who went through Portland are asked about Clive Charles, there's an enormous outpouring of love. In the last months of his life, Clive said that this meant 'everything' to him and that was the reason he had stayed at Portland. He said that the love was reciprocated and that every day he told his players that he loved them. He confessed it was something he couldn't hide.

The current and former players that made up Clive's

extended family had demonstrated how they felt about their former coach in no uncertain terms. Most of them were in attendance on 18 September 2002 when Charles was honoured with his lifetime achievement award.

The influence Clive had on the Portland Pilots, as we have seen, was immense. The success of the team during his time there, and the wellbeing of the players under his tutelage, cannot be overstated. Indeed, recognition of Clive's achievements both with the Pilots and nationally stretched way beyond the city of Portland.

Clive was named the women's soccer Coach of the Year in 2002 by *Soccer Buzz*, an online magazine covering and promoting the sport of women's college soccer. Clive won the Far West Region Coach of the Year four times, and was West Coast Conference Coach of the Year seven times. Twenty-eight of his players have been named All-American.

On 8 December 2002, the Pilot women steamrollered through the NCAA playoffs and, in Texas, during a violent downpour, claimed the NCAA Championship, the pinnacle of collegiate soccer in the United States, for the first time in the school's history, beating West Coast Conference rival Santa Clara 2–1 in sudden-death double extra-time. It was the University's NCAA Division I title in any sport and the Pilots' first triumph in seven Final Four appearances.

Many men and women who had played for and worked with Clive had travelled from around the world to be part of the greatest moment of Clive's collegiate coaching career. The stands at that championship field in Texas were like a human history of Clive's time at Portland. They had come to see their *alma mater* win national athletic glory, but they viewed it as the masterpiece and finale to their teacher's work, so in effect they were there for him.

According to Wynne McIntosh, 'Winning lifted a weight from our shoulders,' and Tiffeny Milbrett called Portland's triumph 'the best day of my life, hands down'.

Shannon MacMillan agreed. 'That was one of the most emotional weekends of my life... Hands down, it's the highlight of my career. I don't think there's a man, a programme or a team more deserving than Clive and Portland... There was nothing better than seeing Clive's face.'

And, after Christine Sinclair's golden goal, Kelly Gray said, 'His face said it all.'

The Cup Final victory was the highlight of Clive's career at Portland. He accepted a lift home in the private jet of Harry Merlo, and the coach apparently sat the whole journey with a wide smile on his thinning face, his arms hugging the trophy.

Portland finished the year with 19 wins, four draws and three losses, and sophomore striker Christine Sinclair was recognised as one of the premier collegiate soccer athletes, leading the nation with 26 goals.

Midfielder Lindsey Huie was named the WCC Freshman of the Year and a first-team Soccer America Freshman All-American. It had been a fantastic year for the Pilots and the best ever in soccer terms for Clive Charles, but he deflected all praise on to his current and former players – crediting the latter for building the programme.

Anson Dorrance, head women's soccer coach at the University of North Carolina, Chapel Hill, said after the Pilot's victory, 'Him winning that National Championship, there wasn't a coach out there who didn't want him to win.'

Jerry Smith, head coach of the Santa Clara University women's soccer team, had been one of the first people to congratulate Clive Charles after the Pilots had beaten Pennsylvania State University in the semi-finals. He recollected with some amusement, 'I said, "Clive, I could not be happier for you and your team making it to the Championship game. We're about to defeat North Carolina in the semi-finals and, when we do, we're going to kick your butt in the finals."

'The moment the ball went into the goal against Santa Clara, I was really disappointed for my team, I was disappointed for my players, I was really heartbroken for my seniors, and one moment after that I couldn't have been happier for Clive Charles.

'He and I shared a nice embrace and a moment and brief conversation within 15 seconds of that ball going into that goal... If Santa Clara wasn't going to win the National Championship, I would want Portland to win it because of my good friend Clive Charles and everything that he's been through.'

Clive was honoured with a Lifetime Achievement Award from the WUSA and awarded an honorary degree from Portland University, both in 2002. In mid-August 2003, he was inducted into the Oregon Sports Hall of Fame for his lifetime achievements as a player and a coach, but he was unable to attend the induction.

Portland's triumph did not escape the notice of the

Oregon political elite who, on 14 February 2002, brought Clive's achievement to national attention. In Washington, a resolution sponsored by US Senators Ron Wyden (the Democratic representative for Oregon) and Gordon Smith (his Republican colleague) congratulated the Pilots for winning the school's first NCAA Championship in any sport, by way of victory in the 2002 NCAA Division I National Championship. The resolution won unanimous approval from the Senate.

Wyden announced, 'Not only is the women's soccer team the first to bring home a National Championship in any sport for the University of Portland, but it overcame steep odds to do it... Climbing from the eighth-seeded team to defeat seven nationally ranked opponents – including the reigning champs – and win the National Championship, these women deserve our congratulations and pride for their tremendous accomplishment.'

'Oregon takes pride in the team's impressive accomplishment,' said Smith. 'Their success on the field is the culmination of determination and sheer talent combined with the outstanding leadership of soccer legend Clive Charles.'

As well as praising the Pilots' accomplishment, Wyden recognised that the 'Title IX' law had laid the basis for equal opportunity in collegiate sports. The Title IX law states that: 'No person in the United States shall, on the basis of sex, be excluded from participation in, be denied the benefits of, or be subjected to discrimination under any education programme or activity receiving Federal financial assistance.'

Wyden stated, 'In this day when Title IX of the Education

Amendments is under challenge, we cannot forget… before Title IX was enacted in 1972, only 1 in 17 high-school girls played team sports – now that number is 1 in 2.5. Title IX has helped our nation develop fantastic athletes like the young women I am here to congratulate. We must continue to encourage these athletes, and provide them with our full support.'

The resolution passed by the Senate highlighted not only the exploits of the women's soccer team and the leadership of head coach Clive Charles, but also the indispensable role of each player, coach, trainer and manager, and the commitment and pride of the University of Portland's students, alumni, faculty and supporters. The coaches and members of the 2002 women's soccer team received a copy of the official resolution from the Senate.

Subsequently, Clive was invited with the team to the White House by President George Bush. Clive's response was typically disarming: 'It'll be the Queen of England asking us to Buckingham Palace next!'

Clive's love for the Pilots programme he built never got in the way of what he saw as his players' best interests. Unlike many college coaches, Charles didn't falter in his guidance of his best players when the professional ranks called. Keller, Steve Cherundolo, Casey, Gray and Nate Jaqua all left after their sophomore or junior years, under Clive's council and tutelage.

Charles was named Grand Marshal of the Grand Floral Parade at the Rose Festival, along with the 2002 National Champion women's soccer team. This event is an awe-inspiring occasion with all-floral floats bringing fantasy to life for half-a-million spectators over a 4.3-mile parade route.

Occurring in June of each year, the festival is Oregon's largest single-day spectator event. The parade boasts the country's largest permanent marching band, beautifully decorated equestrian units, and culturally rich performances in grand style. Captivating generations since 1907, this internationally distinguished parade has been recognised by the International Festival & Events Association and *USA Today* as one of the top five parades in America.

Every year, the Rose Festival president designates an individual or individuals as Grand Marshal of the Grand Floral Parade. Former honourees include film-maker Will Vinton, Senator Mark O Hatfield, retired Oregon Symphony conductor James DePriest, golfer Peter Jacobsen and the Portland Police Department.

I was given a video film by Clive's family showing him and Clarena heading the parade in the back of a bright-red, open-topped Cadillac bedecked with flowers. He looked thin and weak, but the smile never left his face.

Weeks before Clive's induction into the Oregon Sports Hall of Fame, his former club Portland Timbers had announced that they were going to retire his number 3 uniform at the final match of the season on Friday, 29 August 2003, in a half-time ceremony. However, on Tuesday, 26 August, surrounded by family at his home in North-West Portland, Oregon, Clive Charles passed away at the age of 51.

Although he wasn't to see his old number 'raised to glory', when he heard of the intention, he said, 'To know that the number 3 will hang from the rafters permanently is unbelievable to me. To this date, I can remember what it felt like to put that jersey on before every game. I sincerely wish my friend Bobby Howe all the best, and my sincere thanks go out to the Timbers and the Portland soccer community.'

Clive's son Michael, who lettered in golf at the University of Portland (he tutored the game in the Portland area), and his daughter Sarah, a child psychologist and school counsellor, attended the event and heard the huge expressions of goodwill felt for their father.

For the first time in their short A-League history, the Portland Timbers were playing a match that began with the Timbers already eliminated from the playoff race, having been beaten 3–1 by the El Paso Patriots, the previous weekend in Texas. However, it was that same El Paso team that were visiting PGE (Portland General Electric) Park on what was Clive's evening; his spirit breathed through the atmosphere and the Timbers' supporters had spelled out 'CHARLO' (Clive had carried the same nickname into American soccer that was given to his brother John in England) in scarves on the dugout in front of section 107, the domain of the most diehard Timbers' supporters.

The number 3 had been painted in the middle of the park. The board that everyone knew held Clive's number 3 was hanging in the north-east corner of the stadium, just under the roof, but it was still covered at this point. The Timbers wore black armbands on their left sleeves and, before the match kicked off, both teams stood silently on the pitch in a moment of respectful silence.

At half-time, Timbers general manager Jim Taylor stepped to the podium to start the rememberance proceedings. Most of the members of the current Timbers squad had remained on the field for the ceremony, sitting quietly behind the touchline beyond the advertising boards.

Taylor spoke about what Clive had done for the Timbers franchise. This was followed by Timbers captain and former Portland Pilot Brian Winters reflecting on the impact Clive had made on his life. He expressed his thanks to Clive on behalf of all of the Pilots players he had coached over the years.

Former Portland Timber Bill Irwin, who, like Clive, had played for Cardiff City in the English Football League, and had been Clive's assistant almost as long as Clive had been the Pilots coach, spoke of his former team-mate and good friend. After Bill had concluded, Timbers head coach Bobby Howe spoke of what Clive had meant to the team and the city, saying, 'The retiring of Clive's jersey is a fitting testament to not only an outstanding player and true professional, but also to a colleague and a great friend... He has been an inspiration to all players that have had the privilege of playing for him, not only at the University of Portland, but also at club and national team levels.'

During the speeches that followed, Clive's son Michael was also on the field, appearing understandably sombre and, after completing their contributions, each speaker embraced him.

After Bobby Howe had spoken, Jim Taylor announced the official retirement of Clive's number 3; the gesture was the first of its kind in the nearly 80-year history of PGE Park and, as those present turned their eyes to the north-east corner of the stadium, a white banner slowly fell and Clive's 3 uniform was unveiled, along with the years that he had played for the

Timbers: 1978–1981. The crowd rose as one in a standing ovation which lasted for the best part of a minute. Taylor said, 'It only seems fitting that the first-ever retired jersey to hang in the rafters of PGE Park belongs to Clive.'

In the same year Clive joined the Timbers, the team also hired Jim Serrill, better known to all Timbers fans as 'Timber Jim', who continued to act as the Timbers' mascot and one of their biggest fans 25 years later. Timber Jim, at the age of 49, was still climbing the pole and sawing off pieces of the log after each Timbers goal.

A few weeks previously, on 16 August, while the world was watching news of the major blackouts that affected the north-east of the United States, an article quietly slipped out on Oregon Live's website (largely disabled by the blackout), and in the *Oregonian*, stating that Timber Jim was retiring. It was also announced that Timber Jim would not be returning for the final three home games, as he had taken a job in Seattle that would only allow him to get back to Portland at the weekends.

But the evening of 29 August 2003 at PGE Park would not have been complete without Timber Jim and, as the game began, he was there, proudly leading the cheers of the crowd and firing up his chainsaw, just as he had done in the days when Clive Charles played in the Timbers defence.

After Clive's retired jersey had been unveiled, Jim Taylor announced that Timber Jim would be sawing a piece off the log in Clive's honour, and just as he had done hundreds of times before, Timber Jim sawed the last few inches off a log that was set up behind the north goal, and brought the piece out to midfield and presented it to Michael Charles, who held the piece aloft as the crowd once again rose to their feet in applause. Michael himself then went to the podium and spoke of his father, but the emotion of the evening seemed to be overwhelming him by this point, and he spoke only briefly. But his love for his father was very apparent, and it was evident from the moist eyes of those around him and throughout the stadium that many thousands of Portlanders and people throughout the soccer world felt like they had just lost a family member.

The match kicked off and El Paso were caught off guard by Bryn Ritchie, who put the Timbers 1-0 up at the end of the first half. In the second 45 minutes, former Portland Pilot Scott Benedetti fittingly scored the second goal of the evening for the Timbers. With six minutes of the match remaining, Jake Sagare netted for Portland, enabling a fitting 3-0 to be emblazoned on the scoreboard. The '3' shone out significantly over the park.

The Timbers' Army and other Timbers fans presented Timber Jim with a number of mementos, including a trophy fashioned from a cut log with Jim proudly standing on a pole atop the trophy (with the log having been signed by most of the regular Timbers' Army supporters) and a handmade green-and-yellow Timbers axe, together with a photo of Timber Jim signed once more by the Timbers' Army supporters.

For many Timbers fans, saying goodbye to two of the most enduring symbols of the Portland Timbers, and of soccer in the Rose City, could have been a moment of great sadness. But, instead, it defined itself as a time of joyful memories for the spectators. Afterwards, many of the Timbers' Army supporters remained to meet the players, the coaches and Timber Jim. The atmosphere was one of great appreciation that Clive Charles had been central in making Portland a 'soccer city' in the USA. Clive had achieved this through his playing career, his school soccer academy work (where he oversaw all team and player education and development) and as a coach at the city's University; he had poured his heart and soul into the beautiful game, and made it thrive in his adopted home. Portland has some of the most loyal soccer supporters in America, and this had much to do with the spark Clive lit, to create an ember that grew to the flame which continues to burn to this day.

On 29 August 2003, the Portland Timbers broke their A-League single-game attendance record with a crowd of 13,351. It was also the largest crowd the A-League had seen that season. When the crowd had melted away, Clive's number 3 shirt fluttered gently in the breeze, acting as a reminder of a legendary soccer player, coach and a lifetime of achievement.

It was not only in Portland that Clive's life was remembered and celebrated that day. The following was read before the Clemson–South Carolina women's soccer match: 'One of the most influential coaches in our country lost a two-year battle with cancer last week. Please stand and join us as we pause for a moment of silence, in honour and memory of Clive Charles. Clive Charles was an inspiration to players, coaches and educators alike. Although his legacy will live on, we will miss him dearly.'

Just before he died, Clive quietly returned to England and his native roots in the East End of London. He was there to say his final goodbyes to family and close friends. He stayed at the house of his sister Rita, in Collier Row, on the West Essex border of London's Docklands, no more than a dozen miles from where Clive and his brothers and sisters were born and grew up. Visitors to Rita's home during that visit included former West Ham team-mates Frank Lampard, Harry Redknapp and Brian Dear.

It had been a sad 12 months for the Charles family. A year and six days before Clive died, his elder brother and fellow former Hammer, John, the first black professional to play for West Ham, also died of cancer.

John, his wife Carol and their family had made several visits to Clive and his family in America. Carol and John told me about the last occasions they had spent with John's 'little brother', with Carol saying, 'Our Clive had this beautiful beach house on Cannon Beach in the States... we stayed there. Anyway, we went out one day after dinner... we walked for about two minutes and John had to sit on a bench. We walked for about an hour-and-a-half, about four miles... When we came back, he was still sitting on the bench. Clive said he looked like Forrest Gump!'

One of John's sons, Mitchell, told me, 'When we found out about Clive, it shook Dad up... he told me Clive was ill, with cancer. He seemed very quiet about it. He kept a lot of his emotions to himself. But you could see it affected him. They were alike in different ways. They both liked good food... their ways were very alike. They even looked alike.'

For a time, both John and Clive knew they were each simultaneously fighting against cancer like the true East End boys they were. Clive was able to be at John's bedside just days before his brother passed on. He left John with this message: 'These last few months have been difficult for both of our families and us. It would be so easy to feel sorry for ourselves, to say "Why us?"… to give in, to stop trying. But that is not our way. We both have so much to live for.

'John, I think of you every day. I've never told you this before, but, when I was young, you were my hero. I love you very much. Keep your chin up. Keep a smile on your face. Your little brother, Clive.'

John died peacefully on 17 August 2002.

After Clive had also lost his battle with cancer, his long-time assistants Bill Irwin and Garrett Smith respectively took charge of the University of Portland's teams. Both retained their titles as 'assistant' coaches. The University had not determined whether the programmes would continue to have one head coach or a different coach for each team, but there was poetry in the irony… no one could replace Clive.

Of course, condolences flooded in. The famed Head Mentor of the University of North Carolina women's soccer programme Anson Dorrance spoke for many involved in soccer when he remembered, 'He was always very gracious after every match, regardless of the outcome. He didn't change his demeanour. He wasn't catatonic if he lost a game and arrogant when he won one. He was just a very gracious man and that's the way you win respect in our profession, the way you handle yourself in triumph and defeat.'

Dorrance also described Clive's work with the men's Olympic team as inspiring. 'I was just so impressed with the job that he did with our Olympic team in Australia... They played some of the most attractive soccer I've ever seen an American team play.'

US Soccer president Dr S Robert Contiguglia said, 'Clive will be remembered as much for what he accomplished on the field, as what he did off the field... He was a man who developed the game in every significant way possible in this country, from his playing days in the NASL straight through to the development of young athletes on both the men's and women's side of the sport. More importantly, he was a friend, a guide and a mentor to all of those who were touched by his kindness and generosity. While his presence will be truly missed, his spirit will continue to echo throughout the lives of those who knew him.'

For US men's national team manager, Bruce Arena, 'Clive Charles was instrumental in the progress of soccer in the United States on both the men's and women's side of the game... His contributions at both the collegiate and national team levels speak for themselves. He will be sorely missed, and we express our deepest sympathies to his family.'

Bob Howe, ex-Hammer, coaching contemporary and virtual neighbour of Clive's in the States, remembered Clive as being very popular in Portland. He has said publicly that few have equalled 'Charlo's' success in coaching both men and women; it is a very rare talent, although Clive did it seemingly effortlessly. As Bob said, 'You only had to see the accolades he received from players and others to know how well he did.'

According to Portland's director of athletics, Joe Etzel, Clive would 'never be replaced... We're just going to have to do the best we can in his absence.'

For Portland Timbers general manager Jim Taylor, 'No one in soccer has touched and enriched more lives in Portland than Clive Charles... He was a tenacious defender on the pitch, a world-class mentor and coach, and as kind and giving a man as you'll ever know... He has done more for the sport of soccer in Oregon than anyone ever has or ever will. He is the consummate professional, a first-class human being and a person that we all owe a huge debt of gratitude to. He is truly an inspiration to us all.'

Jerry Smith, head coach of the Santa Clara University women's soccer team, admitted it would be odd to play against Portland and not see Clive across the field from him. 'The number of times we would look over at each other and just have a smile, or a shrug of the shoulders or a raise of the eyebrows... I will really miss that because I don't have that with many of my colleagues... Portland will always remain my second favourite women's college team, and it always will be because of Clive.'

Kasey Keller added, 'Clive was probably one of the closest people that I had in my life. For me, it's hard to believe that he is no longer there to be a part of it. Him not being there any more is very difficult.'

Shannon MacMillan observed, 'He said his form of cancer was treatable, but not curable. He was such an incredible person that it didn't change him at all... It only helped us see what an incredible fighter he was.'

Loren Wohlgemuth, a former sports information director at Portland who worked with Clive for seven years, recollected how off the soccer field Clive was not adverse to enlivening the day with some humour. 'He would walk into your office and, if you weren't there, he would grab a sticky note and draw a little cartoon – it was usually "off colour" – and hide it somewhere so a couple of days later you would find it… You knew it was him. He was the practical joker in the building.' She added that Clive was always making side-bets with people, for instance wagering a quarter that he could spit his gum into a garbage can 25ft away, or betting a milkshake that he could kick a ball into a goal from a ridiculous distance. 'There was always somebody who would take him up on it and they would always lose,' Wohlgemuth said.

But perhaps one of the most telling of remembrances of Clive came by way of the work of Alberto Salazar, one of the all-time great marathon runners. His son Alejandro was mentored and guided by Charles through university soccer and Alberto started a website where admirers of Clive shared stories. One told of the 1988 men's Final Four game between Portland and Indiana. The game was deadlocked and scoreless at half-time. In the Pilots' locker room, Coach Charles called for silence. For 15 minutes, he and his players eavesdropped on the tirade of Indiana's coach in the next room. Finally, Charles told his team, 'Go out and keep doing what you're doing… and have fun.'

Clive's family held a private funeral service for the great husband and father who died far too young. Unlike his brother

John, he was never to be compensated with the joy of grandchildren. But, like John, he'd have been a great granddad.

For their coach, the University of Portland organised a memorial service at 3.00pm on 8 September 2003 that was held in Chiles Center, part of the University campus and sporting facilities. At the ceremony, Bill Irwin said, 'We grieve for Clive's family and his thousands of friends at the University and around the world who have lost a generous and sensitive friend... He loved the game, the game was his passion... He really cared about his players and tried to help them in any way he could, no problem was too trivial... He wanted to make them better players and people.'

The University's senior vice-president, Rev E William Beauchamp, added, 'Clive's life and work were gifts of extraordinary worth, and his impact as teacher and coach, friend and mentor, will be felt... for many years to come.'

Clive's contribution to soccer in the USA was massive. The impact he had on both the US men's and women's national teams, as well as MLS, WUSA and countless University of Portland players, was arguably the greatest legacy left to world football by any player or coach that has gone through the West Ham system. He is certainly up there with John Lyall, Ron Greenwood, Malcolm Allison, Noel Cantwell and Bobby Moore, yet he has hardly received the credit he deserves. It is hard to think of any British black player who has achieved so much over such a long period of time and, as such, it is difficult to understand why his contribution is not more widely understood and celebrated.

Many people who knew or met Clive were convinced that

he was going to beat cancer. For most Portland soccer fans and former players, the announcement of his death didn't seem real. Wynne McIntosh appeared to feel this way, saying, 'We've always thought of Clive as sort of invincible. Then you start to think, What if it got to the point where we have to lose Clive? We can't lose Clive!'

And Justi Baumgardt-Yamada recalled, 'The last time I talked to him he sounded good… I spoke to his daughter the other day. She said he has such a great attitude.'

It just didn't seem that Clive was a person who could or should be taken from this world. In many ways, the future was to prove that he wasn't. While cancer has taken his physical presence from the sidelines, it's clear from what his former players say about him that he will always be a part of their lives. The day Clive died, Tiffeny Milbrett and Shannon MacMillan were selected for the US roster for the Women's World Cup.

Clive's continued influence has also been assured by the Charles family, who established the Clive Charles Foundation to help fund cancer research. For them, of course, football was always a background. Clive was a good, caring, loving husband and father, a giver of bear hugs and laughter, with boundless generosity.

With infectious enthusiasm, Clive fought his way through his three-year campaign against multiple cancers, while defying the prognosis that his cancer would kill him within months. In his un-American language and in his Cockney accent, he professed that winning wasn't everything. He was always gracious, articulate and honest. These qualities are why he was so beloved by his players and why his death is such a loss for soccer. This is perhaps Clive Charles's most fitting epitaph – football, yes, but played and taught with love.

Charles was a great ambassador for the game of soccer at all levels for both men and women and had a deep understanding of the game, its gifts and possibilities. He was considered one of the finest people in American soccer, loved by his players, revered by his peers, and respected for his gentle demeanour and intense passion for the sport.

It was in 1995 that Charles, by then recognised as an eloquent speaker, addressed the men's Championship banquet. Knowing how moments of glory can merge into the mists of time, he asked student athletes from all four participating teams to consign consciously the moment they took to the field to long-term memory.

Following Clive's death, Portland University decided to build the Clive Charles Soccer Complex, in memory of their greatest-ever coach, but also to continue the work he started. It was estimated that the cost of the development would be around $1.8 million. In 2004, one of the first initiatives of the project was completed. Floodlights were installed at Merlo Field (now designated as part of the Clive Charles Soccer Complex), allowing night games to be played for the first time in school history. A crowd of 4,070 showed up at the inaugural night match, a 4–0 victory over Weber State on 10 September. It seems fitting that one of the first developments at Portland since Clive's death involved the bringing of light into darkness.

Charles was a surprising, challenging and, at times, uproariously funny man. He could be stubbornly insistent in a motivational way. The edge of his almost impatient energetic keenness was tempered by his inherent patience as a teacher. He was capable of being blunt and even abrupt in his honesty, but could wrap the same in his endearing wit, that sometimes ran at the speed of light. He was a friend to many and he made relationships with those who made up the teams he tended that endured long past playing days.

I have followed Clive's career from afar, and have modelled much of my own teaching style and attitude on his example. I know it to have brought quality to my life and those I have had the honour of working with as a teacher and tutor.

Jeff Gadawski played for and coached with Clive and went on to become president of the FC Portland Academy, the community programme inspired by Clive Charles. He remembered Clive as 'a teacher who used soccer to teach life'.

This is perhaps the greatest tribute a coach can have. The moment the game moves beyond the pitch, it has its reason to be. It becomes more than 'just a game'. Clive used football to help people make themselves 'better' as human beings; he used soccer to enhance humanity. That was his great gift and the greatest gift football can bestow.

It is no accident that soccer tournaments are quests for cups. Of course, most people never get to so much as touch these trophies; some never even see them, except perhaps as images on television or in magazines. The competition for the cup is an echo of the ancient quests for the Holy Grail, the purpose of which was never actually to find that unobtainable object, but to learn and grow from the trials and tribulations undergone during the endless search; the point of questing for the Grail was not the getting of it, but how one went about the attempt; it was a finding of self.

In Clive's time, Portland became Camelot to his King Arthur and his teams were the Knights of the Round Table. All were ostensibly involved in the quest for the material glory of championships by winning games, but at base their shared project was what the great American psychologist Carl Rogers called 'becoming', the united process of being all we can be.

As a youth worker in the East End of London and across the world, I have tried to incorporate this into my own work. Seldom is it the case that what we are doing is entirely about just that, for its own sake. When we're singing, playing football or even going down the pub, it also involves us 'becoming', making ourselves in the process of living.

These days, as a lecturer involved in training what we now call 'informal educators', I find that it is more and more difficult to put over this point to those involved in what is increasingly an instrumental educational system, heavily focused on 'skilling up' and certification. But taking inspiration from the likes of Clive Charles helps. He might be pleased to think his influence has gone full circle and is still working in the place where he grew up and learned his football... I hope so.

The boy from Canning Town was the greatest coach in more than a century of University of Portland athletics, but Clive Michael Charles was a man who prized development over victory; despite this, he was one of America's most successful coaches. He was not only among the most talented and creative individuals in the history of soccer in the United States, he was also the most loved of teachers and coaches. In August 2003, the American and world soccer community lost a great coach and teacher, but it gained a legend and an exemplary role model. Clive's legacy rose above all the scandal and silliness of the modern game to demonstrate the way a person can develop and grow in dignity and integrity through the sport that Clive loved as a child and dedicated himself to as a coach and mentor, having grown up in the same place and time as I did, just a mile or so down the road from West Ham United's Upton Park home.

7

THE STATE OF SOCCER –
BACK TO THE FUTURE

Perhaps the greatest obstacle the NASL faced in the late 1960s was the deficit of players born or developing in the USA and Canada in the rosters of the participating teams. Foreign coaches employed by the clubs had not favoured North American players, looking to men whom they knew and who could offer the experience needed for top-class soccer. Knowing that this was no way to lay the ground for the future of the game in America, the NASL stipulated that all clubs had to field at least one North American player throughout the duration of any given game. The rule worked well and, slowly, the numbers of 'home-grown' players in the league increased. These young men understood the need to make the grade and laid the groundwork for what have become the recognisable traits of American soccer players at the highest level – an ability to work hard, hone their fitness, operate as a team and offer a remarkable standard of commitment.

Overall, as time passed, they began to stand out among the imports, most of whom had seen their best days as players, and/or had come to America for a sort of working holiday. However, this culture of foreign players continued and was among causes of the ultimate decline of the NASL.

Spectators, very often families, paid their hard-earned money to see the foreign players, having had their expectations heightened by the almost rabid promotional machine that surrounded these individuals. All too often, the poorly motivated, unfit and over-the-hill performers didn't live up to the hype, leaving the crowds to walk away from games disappointed and feeling cheated, with no incentive to come back for more of the same. At the same time, these players had a part in killing the goose that laid the golden egg; without fans, there were no fat contracts and no security of tenure.

In time, the NASL policy on home-grown talent achieved unforeseen bonuses; it was from among the ranks of these 'local heroes' that Canada recruited a team capable of taking themselves to the World Cup Finals for the first time in 1986.

From the start, everyone involved in the NASL understood that, to attract an audience, they would need to produce attractive, attacking, entertaining games. To encourage this, a points system was introduced that would reward teams for scoring goals. Regrettably, the endeavour to develop a high level of professional skill on the soccer pitches of North America was initiated during a period when the game was going through one of the most cynical periods in its history; worldwide, top-class soccer seemed to be dominated by unadventurous tactics and the fear of losing. Players, coaches and administrators seemed unable to get away from the defensive approach. As such, even with generous enticements in terms of points, teams stuck with negative strategies.

Sport is a huge enterprise in North America and to grab the interest of the public, both to bring them physically to attend events or to lure them to watch on television, it is necessary to make sure the 'product' offers thrills and drama. Winning is not sufficient, and Americans are not keen on 'ties' or draws either.

Soccer was also a 'foreign' game, in competition with traditional 'American sports' in a merciless market that made every seller fight for the sports dollar. So, combining the high number of players either lacking motivation or carrying an excess of years, an iron-clad culture of defensive play and a cut-throat sports market, the future for soccer looked bleak.

The USA has traditionally adopted a sneering contempt for soccer, and largely dismissed the game as an 'effete', 'effeminate' or 'Limey' pastime, associated with sipping tea and yellow teeth. This attitude was prevalent from the start of the NASL with the American media making it quite clear that soccer was an unwelcome 'alien' and a vaguely unpatriotic interloper into national cultural and sporting life. Prescott Sullivan of the *San Francisco Examiner* was indicative of most of the sports press corps: 'In Europe, as in South America, they go raving mad over the game. Pray that it doesn't happen here. The way to beat it is constant vigilance and rigid control. If soccer shows signs of getting too big, swat it down!'

The common opinion was that America had plenty of sport and didn't need any more, certainly not a game seen to be 'foreign', with rules and regulations that were not understood and terms that were expressed in a vernacular that had clearly been formed without American influence and seemingly impenetrable. The language of soccer and the rules of play had little in common with existing sporting phraseology – the concept of a 'foul', the non-existence of points, the intricacies of penalties, the deep mystery of 'off-side', the fact that the ball could not be handled but that goalkeepers could, as long as they stayed in their 'goal area', and whoever took a 'throw-in'.

Even when the more basic rules were assimilated, the 'off-side rule' still remained, for which there was said to be a 'trap' that people could be 'caught' in or 'left' by it. As a result, coverage of soccer was at best sketchy and often poorly mediated. Even the most determined of would-be fans had to work relatively hard to find out what was going on in the sport or how their team was doing. It was usual for a team's home games to be covered by junior reporters at a local level but reports on away matches hardly ever appeared.

Regardless of the collective apathy and resistance, soccer fought back and, in the mid-1970s, when the New York Cosmos began actively to sign some of the world's top players, public interest seemed to be overcoming the obstacles placed in the path of the game's progress. Other teams followed and, by the late 1970s, many of the greatest exponents of the 'beautiful game' on the face of the planet – the likes of Pelé, Johan Cruyff, Johan Neeskens, Franz

Beckenbauer, Giorgio Chinaglia and Eusébio were with NASL teams. Owners seemed to collect legends as they might baseball cards with an unstoppable momentum.

Growth brought franchises to improbable areas; smaller cities in the USA and Canada began to support professional soccer teams. But the swiftness of the expansion outpaced the financial capacity of the game.

The former Chicago and Toronto general manager Clive Toye saw the rapid growth in 1978 (when seven expansion franchises were admitted to the league) as the prime cause for the NASL's downfall. Of the teams that came into the league after 1977, only Tulsa and Montreal were actually successful in terms of attendances. But, even if this almost frantic augmentation hadn't happened, it is unlikely that the NASL would have survived. Some established clubs, like Minnesota and Portland, were haemorrhaging support prior to the expansion of 1978 and, retrospectively, it appears that North America simply lacked the fan base or the media backing to make the league a success.

Currently, in the United States, more than 10 million children play soccer and a generation has grown up with images and memories of the 'Pelé years'. This represents a significant section of the sports-buying public, but it has taken a quarter-of-a-century to generate, which, in itself, demonstrates that, like most social phenomena, soccer was never going to take root overnight.

The average top English Football League games attract around 24,000 spectators per match; the German Bundesliga, Italian Serie 'A' and Spanish First Division draw about 30,000. Belgian and French First Divisions typically pull in around 10,000–15,000 fans to their games, as the NASL did in its final decade of operation. This appears to corroborate the theory that North America is able to support top-flight professional soccer.

Regrettably, crowds of 10,000–14,000 were not sufficient to maintain megastar names such as Pelé, Beckenbauer and Cruyff. The New York Cosmos were historically the biggest club in the league; they could draw upwards of 40,000 fans per game at the height of their popularity (one year, the average gate was over 48,000), while the ageing Brazilian superstar Pelé played for them. The Giants Stadium sold out (over 73,000) for their 1978 Championship win, while the overall average attendance of the entire league failed to reach 15,000, with some clubs averaging less than 5,000. The probable 'pay the bills' target for most clubs post-1978 was approximately an average attendance of 15,000–20,000. No more than one in three teams achieved that level of support.

After Pelé retired (for the second time) on the conclusion of the 1977 season, there were 18 teams in the league. In 1978, this number grew to 24 and maintained that level of participation for three seasons, until the rapid decline started in 1981.

At the end of the 1970s and start of the 1980s, the golden years of the NASL, attendances to watch the top teams were very encouraging. Crowds for these clubs were on a par with some of the major European teams. But profligacy on international stars (a sin the Cosmos perfected) sent many teams into bankruptcy. As the league dwindled, fan interest shrank.

In 1978, FIFA Secretary Dr Helmut Kaser spoke for the traditional realm of soccer when he accused the NASL of being entirely profit motivated, disregarding the beauty and the laws of the game to that end. FIFA's hostility was based on the NASL's apparently cavalier attitude towards the rules of the game. Faced with the challenge of selling soccer in the USA, the league attempted to 'Americanise' the sport, looking to make soccer more exciting, and understandable, to the American sports fan. Changes to the internationally accepted rules included:

- a clock that counted time down to zero as was usual in other 'time-bound' sports in the USA, rather than upwards to 45 minutes (as was traditional in soccer)
- a 35-yard line for offsides instead of the stipulated halfway line
- a penalty shoot-out to decide matches that ended in a draw
- allowing three substitutes (one extra than allowed generally at the time)
- the generation of a complicated points system applied to wins and losses

FIFA's endeavours to oblige the NASL to comply with the rules that the rest of the world followed were to no avail and it seemed that the Americans thought that messing around with the game was one of their inalienable rights. But the NASL could not intimidate FIFA with the usual American political threat of becoming isolationist; they and the United States Soccer Federation wanted to stage the 1986 World Cup that had originally been awarded to Colombia, before FIFA withdrew their gift after discovering that the South Americans didn't have the infrastructure or stadiums to host the tournament. Bids to step into the subsequent breach came from Canada, Mexico and the USA, but Canada lacked the required stadiums and Mexico had hosted the Cup in 1970. This meant that the United States emerged as the strongest candidate. Henry Kissinger led the US delegation to win the tournament for America (Franz Beckenbauer and Johan Cruyff were other delegates) but the NASL continued to bicker with FIFA.

This ongoing argument perhaps signified the underlying disregard that America felt for soccer. In no other sphere of life did the USA need to negotiate with a political superior. The United States either got its own way or withdrew; it had no record of going cap in hand to world bodies in sport or anything else. In the USA, sport was saturated with patriotism, and two of the underlying principles of American existence are 'freedom' and 'liberty'. For the most part, the idea of having to defer to the authority of a bunch of Europeans and a few South Americans left a bad taste in the mouth of most Americans and, even more so, those with some power and influence within sport, the media or national politics.

The NASL adopted a points system on 21 October 1980 in which goals scored won points. It became possible for a team to earn as many as 15 points for a league victory - 9 for the result, 1 for the first goal, 2 for the second, and 3 points for the third. Four proposed rule changes were also submitted to FIFA for official sanction; the NASL wanted to widen the goal to give more scoring opportunities, ban the back-pass to the goalkeeper, assess penalty time for yellow cards, shorten the length of games to 70 minutes, but introduce time-outs when the ball was out of play.

Phil Woosnam, the NASL Commissioner at the time, reasoned that 'the owners felt this was a way of cutting down on the number of shoot-outs, ties and low-scoring games. This is a way of improving the overall image and quality of the sport in North America.'

Unsurprisingly, FIFA were unimpressed and instructed the NASL to comply with the existing laws of the game, or else the league and the US Soccer Federation would be expelled from FIFA. Having lost the chance of staging the 1986 World Cup and being threatened with being outlawed from world football, the NASL decided rather than capitulate completely to play for time and regroup.

FIFA came to the end of their tether in March 1981. Rene Courte, a FIFA spokesperson, charged the NASL with 'taking us for fools' and informed the league that it 'can't fool around like this'. This was good advice as the refusal to conform would mean that the United States would be excluded from international competitions, club friendlies included, and all those playing in the league would be barred from selection for their national teams.

However, the NASL refused to be intimidated. Vince Casey, a spokesperson for the league, declared, 'We're not running around holding our heads in anguish.'

Just hours before the start of the 1981 season, the NASL appeared to concede and embraced FIFA rules. However, just 13 days later, the NASL announced they would readopt their original rules, alluding to a letter from FIFA President João Havelange that was taken as implicit approval. The NASL maintained that this correspondence gave them an interim endorsement to run the game in North America by their own rules until FIFA determined their suitability for the rest of the planet. US Soccer indicted NASL for 'deliberately misinterpreting' FIFA's position and insisted that Havelange had concurred that this was the case.

This was followed up by the NASL accusing US Soccer of misleading them. Gene Edwards, President of US Soccer, swiftly defended his organisation, saying, 'The statements coming from the league offices are irresponsible and are not an accurate account of the facts. We have done everything in our power to get them the concessions they are asking for.'

The NASL received official notification that their rule changes were not going to be considered on 1 July 1981 and were ordered to revert to FIFA rules with immediate effect. The league reluctantly obeyed and Bob Bell, Chair of San Diego Sockers, expressed the league's view, saying, 'We need major changes in the structure of the game but we can't make them because of FIFA. Every sport makes changes to improve its product. We can't do it, and that's a serious problem.'

FIFA did not consider the USA's bid for the 1986 World Cup, not even making the token effort to set up an inspection committee. Their official explanation for their stance was that the travel time between East and West Coast venues was unacceptable. However, some might have alleged that the actual reason was the brazen conceit of the NASL and the incapability of the US Federation to control the league. The 1986 World Cup was awarded to Mexico for the second time in 16 years.

For the NASL, missing out on the 1986 World Cup was the consequence of a sequence of catastrophic judgements, which was itself part of a series of managerial mistakes that continued the demise and eventual disappearance of the league in the spring of 1985.

As the NASL ploughed through the early 1980s, in open conflict with FIFA, struggling with over-expansion and trying to shift the game indoors in the winter, soccer in America seemed in turmoil. Strong teams like Minneapolis and Montreal were weakened, expansion and relocation didn't work, and the league was still trying to open challenging markets like Toronto.

Even with all the difficulties, soccer was still able to produce some great moments. The likes of the Vancouver Whitecaps and Chicago Sting were capable of demonstrating that, given the right circumstances, North American cities were well able to support teams.

One major factor that compromised the success of some teams during the 1980s, such as Seattle and Minnesota, was the widespread changes in ownership, which often caused a significant downturn in fortunes. Molsons Breweries, for example, who owned the Montreal Manic, played a part in the self-destruction of the club. In the initial two seasons, Manic were often able to attract crowds of more than 20,000, at times they pushed up to 30,000 in the Olympic Stadium. But, before the 1983 season, Molsons made the decision that the Montreal side would be renamed 'Team Canada'; in effect, the Manic would become defunct to be replaced by the Canadian national team that would represent Montreal in the NASL. The numbers attending matches slumped instantly, from an average of 21,000 to little more than 5,000; consequently, the Montreal franchise crashed and burned.

In an attempt to put the brakes on the league's seeming collapse, on 22 June 1982, the former NASL Commissioner Howard Samuels was named president and CEO. In 1967, he had been the Under-Secretary of Commerce in the administration of US President Lyndon Johnson, and he immediately set himself the task of invigorating the NASL and turning it around from a financial and marketing perspective, the very areas where the league had proved most wanting.

For all this, the decline of the NASL went on unabated and, on 26 October 1984, at the age of 64, Howard Samuels, who had worked wonders just keeping the league together, tragically passed away after a heart-attack. His death left a leadership vacuum and a loss of direction. The league lasted just five months longer.

Following Samuels's death, the task of attempting to rescue the NASL was taken up by Clive Toye, who became interim president. As Cosmos manager, he had been the man who had signed the likes of Pelé and Beckenbauer, helping to invigorate the American soccer boom of the mid-1970s. A brief period with the Chicago Sting was followed by a move to the Toronto Blizzard, where he was able to steady the wavering and inadequately supported franchise.

Toye led the Blizzard to appearances in the last two NASL Championships, but was unable to boost the club's attendance figures. However, he acted on his belief that the best was still possible. When he took charge of the Blizzard, the city of Toronto was known as a city that supported their professional sports teams with passion in spite of their sometimes hard luck, but it seemed that the Blizzard was the exception that proved the rule.

Not long after joining the franchise, Toye was able to point to gates of 20,000–30,000 at the old Toronto Exposition Center, supporting one of the NASL's best sides. For Toye, there was 'no question whatsoever in my mind that Toronto should be and could be one of the best, if not *the* best, franchises in the North American Soccer League'.

Toye's forthright confidence was met by plummeting attendances, regardless of how well the Blizzard played or the results they managed. By the midway point in the 1984 season, even Toye had to admit that Toronto were in dire trouble. 'In the past three years, we have removed the reasons always given to us by the fans as an excuse as to why they're not supporting us. People said all winter that they will be behind us now that we have done all those things. They didn't keep their promise and I feel somewhat let down.'

Toye had been with the league for 18 years, through good times and bad, and had long been of the opinion that the NASL had grown too swiftly. Over-expansion had indeed been a major factor in the demise of the league. When the league began to grow, new franchises were swiftly awarded, and the NASL doubled in size within a few years – at its largest, the league boasted 24 teams. It has been argued that cash-strapped established owners were anxious for their share of the expansion fees to be charged to new owners, even though *Forbes Magazine* claimed this amounted to just $100,000. The consequence of this was that talent was thinly spread; in addition to this, though, many of the new owners were not 'soccer people' but mere speculators, and, once the initial popularity of the game began to decrease, they left as quickly as they came.

Toye submitted a 46-page survival plan to the league on 12 September 1984. It proposed a six-team league for 1985, with slow extension over the following decade. It also advised that the season should be made up of a 16-game schedule with a cup competition between the NASL and Mexican club sides. The plan was supported by the remaining league officials, with the Cosmos, Blizzard, Minnesota Strikers and the Vancouver Whitecaps assuring their clubs' participation in the 1985 season.

With these four teams committed, Toye tried to negotiate a merger between Golden Bay and San Diego, at the same time hoping that one of the Major Indoor Soccer League franchises (St Louis or Baltimore) might opt to play outdoors in the NASL. Toye's strategy was 'to bring together the remaining clubs in the NASL, along with those who share our philosophies, to form a valid, common-sense league'.

Early in March, only Toronto and Minnesota would remain in the black, with new ownership attempting to revive the

Tulsa Roughnecks. San Diego and Champions Chicago Sting quit in favour of a move to the MISL. New York were suspended (and also eventually joined the MISL) and Tampa withdrew. With just two teams, the 1985 season became untenable, but Toye was inevitably positive: 'I found in the last 90 days a strong, positive attitude from a number of people in a number of cities, but the problems of the past combined with an extreme shortage of time made it impossible to bring in new members in 1985. It is this positive attitude, however, that makes me believe that professional soccer can be reorganised and restructured and that a good pro league will be in operation for the 1986 season.'

The league tried increasing the Championship from a single game to a three-game series to draw attention, but it was too little, too late. The Chicago Sting defeated the Toronto Blizzard on 3 October 1984 to take the Championship 2–0 in the last NASL game ever played. With just two clubs left to contest the 1985 season, Toye had little option but to suspend activity, conceding that there was scant interest in the league.

The last gasps of the NASL in the first part of 1985 hit the North American game hard. The dream of tens of thousands of players, administrators, fans and owners to create a top-class professional league to operate on a coast-to-coast basis seemed to have died. From 1968, it looked as if soccer was making a place for itself and, following the struggles of those first years, the professional game appeared to have put down roots that showed signs of coming to fruition in the late 1970s and early 1980s. But, apparently unaccountably, it had

245

expired, leaving what felt like a huge void in the future of soccer as a world game – for that to be achieved, the involvement of the USA would be critical.

Looking back on the period of consistent failure prior to the formation of the NASL, it seemed that all hope had gone; if the NASL were unable to survive, how would any heir be successful?

Ironically, as the NASL neared its death throes, soccer in the USA was experiencing one of its most triumphant moments. The crowds who had failed to attend NASL matches in their tens of thousands flocked to watch the 1984 Olympic Games soccer tournament, which was played at four venues; on the east coast in Cambridge and Annapolis, and Palo Alto and Pasadena in the west. After the conclusion of the Games, soccer proved to be the most popular sport, drawing 1,422,000 spectators; that was around 300,000 more than the traditionally favoured track and field. The Rose Bowl Pasadena hosted the Olympic Final and attracted 101,970 people, a record soccer crowd for the USA.

Certainly, these figures were a powerful influence on FIFA gifting the USA the 1994 World Cup Finals. But the 'Olympics effect' endured only as long as the Games. When the USA met Costa Rica at Stanford University in California in the Olympic tournament, 78,265 turned up; only a year later, when the same teams played each other in Los Angeles in a World Cup qualifying game, the attendance was just 11,800.

This situation, together with the failure of the NASL, seemed to indicate that the best soccer could do was to be an occasional and temporary aberration on the American sporting horizon, a novelty act that allowed participation with foreigners from time to time. But, in the main, the great US public preferred to keep their professional sport 'in-house' and fight out baseball and grid-iron football 'world championships' between themselves. It was a sort of 'win/win' dream.

However, for Americans, the Olympics are the ultimate in sport, only challenged by the World Series baseball and grid-iron's Super Bowl. This being the case, many Americans who couldn't get tickets for other Olympic events, but still wanting to be part of the great affair which was the 1984 Olympics, opted to attend the soccer matches that were being staged in massive stadiums that gave a better opportunity to get a ticket than other sports, such as boxing.

Post-Olympics, with the collapse of the NASL still fresh in the collective memory, soccer went through a period of stagnation between 1985 and 1986. But there were a couple of silver linings – Canada made the 1986 World Cup Finals, with players largely developed in the NASL. Then, in 1985, a semi-professional league was formed on the west coast of the United States – the Western Soccer Alliance (WSA).

At first, the WSA appeared to do little more than offer the young players on the west coast an opportunity to play. But, with the formation of the American Soccer League (a third incarnation of this title in the history of soccer in the USA) in 1988 on the east coast, it helped form the basis of a new national league set up along regional lines.

The first authentic national league in Canada was formed in 1987 and, being conscious of the failures of the leagues that had gone before and of all the difficulties posed by travelling huge distances in such a vast nation, the Canadian Soccer League (CSL) shrewdly kept travel to a minimum. It held on to the national profile, though, and, crucially, adopted small, sensible budgetary strategies based on realistic appraisals of attendances.

Dissimilar to former Canadian leagues, the CSL limited teams to three overseas players per club, so giving opportunities for Canadian players to develop. Crowds did not exceed modest levels, as was traditional, but the league got through its inaugural and second years avoiding any serious problems, and started the 1989 season with ten teams.

Many of the players in the CSL had appeared in the NASL and were also members of Canada's 1986 World Cup squad, thus providing the league with immediate integrity. Indeed, the Toronto Blizzard took up their place in the CSL as a former NASL team.

The WSA and the ASL also boasted former NASL names – San José Earthquakes, Washington Diplomats, Tampa Bay Rowdies and Fort Lauderdale Strikers.

All the competitions at this time looked to promote US and Canadian players, an approach which the NASL might have been wise to follow from the beginning.

In its heyday, NASL teams competed against some of the best club sides in the world and often held their own, and even some of the weaker teams were capable of giving European sides a run for their money.

It is true that the history of the NASL was relatively short and even the mighty Cosmos eventually bit the dust; it therefore cannot be denied that the NASL failed. But it did introduce soccer to the North American sports scene on a scale never seen before and was a major factor in the game becoming the principal participatory sport among the youth of the USA. At the end of the 1980s, FIFA did award the World Cup to the USA. The 1994 World Cup proved to be a great shot in the arm for soccer in America. It attracted large crowds and the USA prepared well for the tournament. The national team performed creditably and, it seems, soccer has at last gained a respectable and dedicated following in North America. Recent figures for attendance at MLS games show that, over 192 games, the average attendance was around 15,500, and that a total of nearly 3 million people turned up to watch the games. Many more tuned in on TV. Given these figures, soccer most certainly has a healthy future in the Land of the Free.

The NASL has also provided lessons for its successor; the MLS has taken precautions against the problems the NASL suffered. American college soccer, which has underpinned the success of the MLS, still uses some NASL-style rules.

After 1985, the USA was without a sanctioned First Division for 11 years, but it says much for the legacy of the NASL that American soccer has risen out of the ashes with a history and an experience that can ensure a secure future. The USA has produced male teams able to hold their own in the international arena and a tradition in the women's game that is unmatchable All this has its foundation in the NASL.

8

UNITING BLACK
AND WHITE

It is impossible to capture lives within pages of books but, with some effort, one can convey the ethos of a time, the feeling of place and the power of personality. I think that the lives of the three players highlighted in the previous pages, and the football environment in which they lived and played, tell the reader a great deal about what it is to be a footballer, but also how complex the living of our lives can be. The joys are heightened by the sadness, and what appears to be failure at one point in time can so often become the foundation for success. The world just isn't black and white.

In fact, this book, in that it is also a study of the nature of identity within the football arena, demonstrates how national and racial differences can be subsumed in the process of 'thoughtful living'. In that respect, it seeks to question the traditional analysis of the experience of black footballers in the British game that argues that race is an overriding consideration in terms of forming the identity of soccer professionals.

The portrayal of the experience of black footballers in Britain has been set in the context of this group's position as the target of racism, mainly of an overt type, overwhelmingly emanating from supporters. As a consequence, the black footballer has, under the gaze of the academic and the social reformer, become stereotyped as a victim who must look to the sympathetic (generally white) campaigner to pressurise for legislation to outlaw and socially admonish the persecutors. This vision, which contorts the football stadium into a latter-day Roman arena, with its hapless victims, barbaric persecutors and noble saviours, is built on two models of supposed deficit:

Fans, nearly always described as a minority, are potentially or actually racist, to the extent that there is a need for legislation to arrest the practice and development of racist behaviour. The 'fact' of supporter racism is borne out by the predominantly racial characteristics of those attending football matches – they are overwhelmingly white.

Black footballers, without the 'help' of campaigning groups, mostly made up of white people from professional backgrounds, have been and would be helplessly persecuted by the racism of the supporters, albeit that this is the 'minority'.

There are many flaws in this scenario. This 'football world' has, in the main, been built by those who have migrated into football as its fan base has gentrified. When John Charles, the first 'Black Hammer' took to the field for the West Ham first team back in the early 1960s, there were few social anthropologists standing in the Chicken Run, the traditional stamping ground of West Ham's hardcore supporters, with their tape recorders. In short, the group that have defined racism in football are the successors to the likes of Margaret Mead, the cultural anthropologist – they are outsiders defining the behaviour of 'natives' from a particular standpoint outside of the experience of those being observed (the supporters and players).

Within this situation, the myth arose that 'West Ham is a racist club'. This was particularly prevalent as a notion throughout the 1970s and into the 1980s, and has not entirely been exorcised to this day. It is based on contentions that West Ham, alongside one or two other groups of supporters, gave (and give) black players a much harder time than supporters of clubs of comparable status. Such accusations are familiar to anyone who has been involved in examining and trying to deal with racism in football. West Ham supporters seem to be locked into an association with the club's most infamous supporter, Alf Garnett, the bigot, racist, satirical and surreal creation of local writer the late Johnny Speight. However, the experience of those players contributing to this book questions this set of assumptions, this discrimination and prejudice. Perhaps more importantly, collectively they demonstrate that the experience of black footballers, at least at West Ham, is exceptional relative to their white counterparts, only in terms of their comparatively high degree of success and contribution to the world game. This contradicts much of the academic endeavour of the last couple of decades devoted to the analysis of racism in football.

On 1 April 1973 at Upton Park, Best, Coker and Charles did not experience the kind of greeting that Cyrille Regis, the former electrician from non-league Hayes, got when he broke into the West Bromwich Albion first team within a few months of signing for the club, in May 1977. When recalling the racial abuse that he endured initially from some of the Hawthorns crowd, he said, 'I think they were rebelling against me 'cause I'd taken a white guy's place in the team.'

As their personal recollections testify, the 'Three from '73' remember their time at Upton Park and the crowd with affection and warmth, but this didn't stop them from becoming role models for many black youngsters. Clyde Best, a powerful centre-forward, entered the first team at West Ham in 1969, a time of increasing television coverage of football. His brave and bold striking style was relayed to an audience of black youngsters who had never really seen his like before. A young black footballer remembered Best's influence, saying, 'When I was younger, there weren't any black players. I saw that football was dominated by white players and just run by white clubs, and, when I saw Clyde Best for the first time on TV as a black player, it made me think, Black men can get into the Football League if they work hard enough at it.'

This young man had made a great discovery. I made a

similar discovery while writing this book via the inspiration I gained directly from the three individuals whose lives have been depicted here. Power is not given by well-meaning liberals; the idea that one human being can give power or authority or even respect is the result of contradictory thinking. Clyde Best (like Clive Charles and Ade Coker) took power and this gave him his authority on the field and earned him respect. The power that Clyde had at his disposal was not gained at the behest of some white do-gooder going around 'giving power'; his power came out of his own efforts, self-belief, will and soul. That is where individual power comes from – and from nowhere else!

West Ham have traditionally drawn on the support from those who live within walking distance of the Boleyn Ground. This has changed slightly in the past couple of decades, with many families moving out to the 'far East End', into North and West Essex. However, supporters generally have family and 'roots' connections with the district surrounding Upton Park. The area, taking in the Docklands of East London, has a strong association with socialism and the political Left. The people of the area sent the first Labour MP to Westminster and initiated the first manifestation of radical local government action of the early years of the century, that saw local councillors sent to jail for supporting industrial action.

This background testifies to the fact that the people most closely associated with supporting West Ham United have a history of egalitarian sentiment and a commitment to social justice. This was exemplified again and again as the 20th century wore on, while West Ham United evolved from a works team based in the docks to a top-flight professional club. It was the dock workers, together with gas workers and railway men, who allied themselves with the Jews of the East End to bar Oswald Mosley's black-shirted fascists from entering their patch with the slogan 'They Shall Not Pass!' My own grandfather, a stoker in the West Ham gasworks, stood nose to nose with British Nazis denying them a passage over the Iron Bridge (built by Thames Ironworks) that linked West Ham to the rest of East London, west of Bow Creek.

The same class of people carried on a tradition of trade-union militancy right up to the time when the first black players began to break through at Upton Park. When the British National Party won a council by-election on the Isle of Dogs in the mid-1990s following an extraordinarily low turnout, local people were quick to rid themselves of this embarrassment at the very next opportunity, kicking the BNP member out in the most emphatic fashion.

The Docklands area is, and has been historically, over hundreds of years, one of the most multi-racial in the country. It has played host to successive waves of immigration – Huguenot, Jewish, Chinese, African, Caribbean, Indian, Bengali and, more recently, mid- and East-European refugees. Immigrants have arrived in Britain within earshot of Upton Park and set up families, homes and businesses in the streets abutting 'the home of the Hammers'. The area also boasts significant Italian, Greek, Turkish and Maltese communities. Growing up in the East End of London means being integrated into the most ethnically diverse of environments where differences in language, religion, colour, dress and culture are more an expectation than a provocation.

All this casts doubt on the accusation that West Ham is a club with *particularly* racist support and it is this doubt that motivated the writing of this book. It seems that those who would be the most likely victims of racism at West Ham United, who would be best placed to confirm or deny the level of racism expressed by supporters, were the black players who pulled on the claret-and-blue shirts and wore the Irons next to their hearts.

East End Heroes, Stateside Kings draws on their first-hand experience, and what this shows is that, far from being stunted by racism, the three black men who gave so much of themselves to English and world football grew, bloomed and flourished on the basis of their experiences at Upton Park. They remembered their time there with affection and, from the secure foundation it provided for them, they literally went on to conquer the world. These were not men in need of rescue. Yes, they struggled, but they made their lives happen from the source of their own potential and spirit and drew on the resources offered to them at West Ham. For these pioneering black men, it was a club and a community that nurtured their talent and remembers them with pride and a kind of familial love that each of them felt and recollected with warmth and fondness. In more ways than one, they were and are East End heroes, and they truly became and will remain Stateside Kings.

APPENDIX I

CLIVE CHARLES – CAREER HIGHLIGHTS

MEN'S PROGRAMME – UNIVERSITY OF PORTLAND
10 NCAA playoff berths, 1988-93, 1995, 1999, 2001, 2002
NCAA Final Four, 1988, 1995
Five WCC titles, 1988, 1989, 1990, 1992, 2002
Far West Region Coach of the Year, 1988
WCC Coach of the Year, 1988, 2002
NCSC Coach of the Year, 1988
Portland's First Top-20 Ranking, 1988

WOMEN'S PROGRAMME – UNIVERSITY OF PORTLAND
2002 College Cup Champions
10 NCAA playoff berths, 1992-98, 2000-02
NCAA Final Four, 1994, 1995, 1996, 1998, 2000-02
Six WCC titles, 1992, 1994, 1995, 1996, 1997, 2000
Two NCSC Championships, 1990, 1991

Soccer Buzz National Coach of the Year, 2002

Far West Region Coach of the Year, 1992, 1993, 1995

WCC Coach of the Year, 1993, 1994, 1995

NCSC Coach of the Year, 1990

Portland's First Top-20 Ranking, 1990

Under Coach Charles's leadership, 28 University of Portland athletes have attained All-America status. In the history of collegiate soccer, he is only the second coach to have two teams, in the same year, competing in the NCAA semi-finals.

NATIONAL

Head Coach, US Men's Olympic Team, 2000 (named in 1996)

Assistant Coach, US Men's National Team, 1995–98

Head Coach, US U-20 Women's National Team, 1993–96

OTHER

ESPN television analyst, 1994 World Cup

Oregonian Banquet of Champions: Merit Award, 1992

Slats Gill Coach of the Year Award, 1995, 2002

APPENDIX II

CLIVE CHARLES'S CAREER RECORD

NASL REGULAR SEASON AND PLAYOFFS

	Regular Season			Playoffs		
	GP	G	A	GP	G	A
1971 Montreal Olympics	21	0	1	-	-	-
1972 Montreal Olympics	7	0	0	-	-	-
1978 Portland Timbers	25	0	2	5	0	0
1979 Portland Timbers	29	0	5	-	-	-
1980 Portland Timbers	9	0	4	-	-	-
1981 Portland Timbers	4	0	1	-	-	-
Total	95	0	13	5	0	0

MEN'S RECORD

Won 213, drawn 92 and lost 31 (17 years, win rate of 64 per cent)

WOMEN'S RECORD

Won 226, drawn 52 and lost 13 (14 years, win rate of 78 per cent)

APPENDIX III

THE CLIVE CHARLES SOCCER COMPLEX

At Portland's Merlo Field, a club house is planned; it will be called the Clive Charles Soccer Complex.

To honour Clive Charles's 17 years of the inspirational leadership in collegiate soccer, the University of Portland has established the Clive Charles Soccer Complex on the University campus. The complex brings to life Clive's wish for continued facility development and improvement to provide his talented players with the finest possible environment in which to train and compete at the highest levels of the sport.

The centrepiece of the complex will continue to be the Harry A Merlo Field, built in 1990 and one of the USA's premier soccer venues. Merlo Field will be augmented by new state-of-the-art practice fields, upgraded support facilities and an enhanced stadium for spectators. In addition, a regulation Fieldturf field will be constructed, which will allow year-round practice opportunities. Renovated and enlarged locker rooms will accommodate more efficiently the top collegiate teams that visit the University.

The Clive Charles Soccer Complex will affirm Clive's incomparable legacy at the University and will permanently honour one of the great figures in the University's history.

The Clive Charles Foundation was established in 2003 by Clarena Charles and Clive's long-time friends Portland businessmen Harry Merlo and Earle Chiles.

It was Clive's guiding principle that, through the game of soccer, there was an opportunity to develop and prepare young people for the challenges of life.

The purpose of the Clive Charles Foundation is to carry forward Clive's work in regard to servicing youth development through the game of soccer in Oregon. In addition, the Foundation will aid in the support of cancer research in the hope that, some day, this illness can be prevented.

For further information, please contact the Foundation on (503) 693-2494, or send donations to:

The Clive Charles Foundation
2250 NE 25th Ave
Hillsboro OR. 97124

BIBLIOGRAPHY

Back, L, *The Changing Face of Football*, Crabbe, T and Solomos, J – Berg (2001)

Barnes, J, *John Barnes* – Headline Publishing Group (1999)

Belton, B, *Brown Out* – Pennant Books (2007)

Belton, B & Cuetwynd, J, *British Baseball and the West Ham Club* – McFarland (2007)

Belton, B, *Bubbles, Hammers and Dreams* – Breedon Books (1997)

Belton, B, *Burn Johnny Byrne – Football Inferno* – Breedon Books (2004)

Belton, B, *Days of Iron* – Breedon Books (1999)

Belton, B, *Founded on Iron* – Tempus (2003)

Belton, B, *Johnnie the One* – Tempus (2003)

Belton, B, *The Black Hammers* – Pennant Books (2007)

Belton, B, *The First and Last Englishmen* – Breedon Books (1998)

Belton, B, *The Lads of '23* – Soccerdata (2006)

Belton, B, *The Men of '64* – Tempus (2005)

Belton, B, *The West Ham Miscellany* – Pennant Books (2007)

Belton, B, *War Hammers* – NPI Media Group (2007)

Blows, K and Hogg, T, *West Ham: The Essential History* – Headline (2000)

Bradbury, S, *The New Football Communities*, Sir Norman Chester Centre for Football Research – University of Leicester (2001)

Brown, M, 'Asian Games' in *When Saturday Comes* – February, pp. 14–17 (1995)

Cashmore, E, *Black Sportsmen* – Routledge (1982)

Commission for Racial Equality, PFA, The Football Trust, *Let's Kick Racism out of Football* (1994)

Fenton, T, *At Home with the Hammers* – Nicholas Kaye (1960)

Greenwood, R, *Yours Sincerely Ron Greenwood* – Willow Books (1984)

Ferdinand, L, *Sir Les* – Headline Book Publishing Ltd (1997)

Groves, R, *West Ham United* – London: Cassel & Co (1948)

Helliar, J and Leatherdale, C, *West Ham United, The Elite Era* – Desert Island, 2nd ed. (2005)

Highfields Oral History Group, *Highfield Rangers: An Oral History* – Leicester City Council (1994)

Hill, D, *Out of His Skin: the John Barnes Phenomenon* – Faber (1989)

Hogg, T and McDonald, T, *1895–1995 – Hammers 100 Years of Football* – Independent UK Sports Publications (1995)

Hogg, T, *West Ham United Who's Who*, Independent UK Sports Publications (2005)

Hugman, B, *The PFA Premier & Football League Players*

BIBLIOGRAPHY

Records 1946-2005, Queen Anne Press (2005)

Irving, D, *The West Ham United Football Book* - Stanley Paul (1968)

Irving, D, *The West Ham United Football Book No. 2* - Stanley Paul (1969)

Jose, C, *NASL - A Complete Record of the North American Soccer League* - Breedon Books (1989)

Kerrigan, C, *A History of the English Schools' Football Association 1904-2004* - ESFA (2004)

Korr, C, *West Ham United* - Duckworth (1986)

Leatherdale, C, *West Ham United from Greenwood to Redknapp* - Desert Island (1998)

Leeds TUC and AFA, *Terror on the Terraces* - unpublished monograph (1987)

Longmore, A, 'Black Revolution' in *Football Today* - November pp. 6-7 (1988)

Lyall, J, *Just Like My Dreams* - Penguin (1989)

Moynihan, J, *The West Ham Story* - Arthur Baker Ltd (1984)

Northcutt, J and Shoesmith, R, *West Ham United - A Complete Record* - Breedon Books (1993)

Northcutt, J and Shoesmith, R, *West Ham United - An Illustrated History* - Breedon Books (1994)

Oliver, G, *World Soccer* - Guinness (2nd Ed) (1995)

Parkinson, Shaw and Ticher, 'Part and Parcel of Every Game You Played' in *When Saturday Comes* - August 2001, pp. 26-28, Hill (2001)

Szymanski, S, 'A Market Test for Discrimination in the English Professional Leagues' in *Journal of Political Economy*, Vol.

108, No. 3 (2000)

Tossell, C, *Playing for Uncle Sam - The Brit's Story of the North American Soccer League* - Mainstream (2003)

Vasili, P, 'The History of Black Footballers in Britain' - unpublished paper (1994)

Vasili, P, *Colouring Over the White Line* - Mainstream Press (2000)

Wall, F, *Fifty Years of Football*, Cassel & Co (1935)

Walvin, J, *The People's Game - A Social History of British Football* - A Lane (1975)

Walvin, J, *Football and the Decline of Britain* - Macmillan (1986)

Ward, A, *West Ham United 1895-1999* - Octopus (1999)

Westwood, S, 'Racism, Black Masculinity and the Politics of Space' in *Men, Masculinities and Social Theory* - Hearn, J and Morgan, D (eds), Unwin and Hyman, pp. 55-71 (1990)

Wigglesworth, N, *The Evolution of English Sport* - Frank Cass (1996)

Williams, J, *Is It All Over? Can Football Survive the FA Premier League?* - South Street Press (1999)

Williams, J, *'Lick My Boots…' Racism in English Football* - SNCCFR, Leicester University (1992)

Woolnough, B, *Black Magic: England's Black Footballers*, London (1983)

Journals/Newspapers
Daily Mail
Ex Magazine
Hammers News